Lahore

The historical record of the 5th Punjab Infantry

Lahore

The historical record of the 5th Punjab Infantry

ISBN/EAN: 9783744640572

Printed in Europe, USA, Canada, Australia, Japan

Cover: Foto ©ninafisch / pixelio.de

More available books at **www.hansebooks.com**

THE

HISTORICAL RECORD

OF THE

5TH PUNJAB INFANTRY,

PUNJAB FRONTIER FORCE.

"Peiwar Kotal,"—"Charasia,"—"Kabul, 1879,"—
"Afghanistan, 1878-80."

By Authority.

LAHORE:
PUNJAB GOVERNMENT PRESS,
1887.

CONTENTS.

CONTENTS.

HISTORY

OF THE

5TH REGIMENT PUNJAB INFANTRY,

PUNJAB FRONTIER FORCE.

THE regiment was raised at Leiah in 1849. The following were the English officers originally posted to it :— Regiment raised.

    Captain J. E. Gastrell, 13th Bengal Native Infantry, Commandant.

    Lieutenant G. W. G. Green, 2nd Bengal Fusiliers, 2nd-in-Command.

    Lieutenant W. McNeile, 5th Bengal Native Infantry, Adjutant.

In March 1850 the regiment received arms, percussion muskets, and was brought on the roster of duty. The detachment of the Line, which had hitherto taken the duties of the station, was consequently withdrawn. Arms received.

In April 1850 the regiment marched from Leiah to Dera Gházi Khan ; companies were detached, one to Mithankote and one to Jhung. The latter was withdrawn in May 1851. Marches to Dera Ghazi Khan.

In November 1850 the composition of the regiment was as follows :— Composition of regiment.

Sikhs of all ranks	...	...	86
Other Punjabís ditto	...	...	454
Hindustánis ditto	...	...	360
	Total	...	900

In January 1851 the regiment was inspected by Brigadie J. S. Hodgson, Commanding the Force. Inspection of regiment.

In March 1851 the left wing, under the command of Lieutenant Green, was ordered to Asnee. Left wing ordered to Asnee.

Changes in equipment.

January 1852.—Up to this period the regiment had been dressed and equipped like the regiments of the Line of the Bengal Army, but with black leather cross-belts of the description issued to local corps. This equipment now underwent some change, the white linen jackets and trousers provided for summer wear in particular being found quite unsuitable for a regiment taking the rough duties of the Deraját frontier. A dyed linen jacket and trousers were therefore substituted, and each man was further required to keep up a "khaki" smock and pyjamahs for service and fatigue duties.

Regiment inspected.

In February 1852 the regiment was inspected by Brigadier Hodgson, Commanding the Force.

Regiment commences to take the frontier post duties.

In March 1852, the line of frontier outposts having been established, the regiment was called upon to furnish the infantry parties at each of the 16 posts from Kin up to Vehowah, a distance of 200 miles. This duty, though harassing and uninteresting, afforded a useful training to the non-commissioned officers and men, particularly to the former, and gave them an insight into their duties and responsibilities, the benefit of which has since been very observable.

March of a company from Mangrotah to Vehowah.

On the occasion of the raid of the Kesráni tribe on Dera Fatteh Khan in March 1852, No. 5 Company, which was then at Mangrotah, was directed to march at once to Vehowah. The company, under Subadár Umrao Misser, marched in the evening, and accomplished the entire distance, 30 miles, during the night, in spite of bad roads and heavy rain. After a halt of one day at Vehowah the company returned to Dera Gházi Khan, 90 miles, in three marches, with the camp of Sir Henry Lawrence, K.C.B., President of the Board of Administration.

Regiment complimented.

The regiment was afterwards complimented by Brigadier Hodgson for the rapidity with which this and other marches on the frontier were executed.

Inspected by Sir Henry Lawrence.

In March 1852 the regiment paraded for the inspection of Sir Henry Lawrence, K.C.B.

Regimental transport completed.

March 1852.—About this time the regimental transport was completed—70 camels and 40 mules. The former were chiefly purchased in the Dera Gházi Khan district, the mules in the Jhelum and Ráwalpindi districts, and a few in Upper Scind.

In May 1852 the regiment volunteered for service in Burma. The offer was acknowledged by the Governor-General in the following terms :— *The regiment volunteers for service in Burma.*

"The Governor-General has perused with great satisfaction the account of this manifestation of loyal and soldier-like feeling on the part of the men, but His Lordship in Council is precluded, on account of the distance at which they are placed and the frontier on which they are engaged, for employing them in Burma." *Thanks accorded by the Governor-General.*

In August 1852 colours were received and delivered to the regiment. *Colours received.*

In February 1853 orders were received for changing the uniform of the regiment from red to "khaki" (drab). *Change in uniform.*

In April and May 1953, while in general command of the Infantry frontier outposts, Jemadár Sohan Tewary, with the post of Mahoee, made a successful pursuit of a body of marauders, and recovered all the cattle they had driven off. *Successful pursuit of marauders.*

In June 1853 the threatening attitude of the Murree tribe caused the prompt despatch of an additional company to Asnee. It marched from Dera Ghází Khan at 9 P.M. of one day, and reached Asnee in three (3) marches : the distance is 96 miles. *Asnee reinforced and forced march of a company.*

In July 1853 the composition of the regiment was as follows :— *Composition of the regiment.*

Hindustánis of all ranks	...	246
Sikhs and Punjabis ditto	...	565
Trans-Indus men ditto	...	95
Total	...	906

In July 1853 the regiment was employed on several occasions, at the requisition of the civil authorities, in repairing and strengthening the bunds in the vicinity of the town and cantonment consequent on the overflowing of the Indus. The thanks of Government were afterwards accorded to the regiment for the zealous and efficient assistance given on these occasions. *Regiment employed in fatigue duty. Regiment accorded the thanks of Government.*

Lieutenant G. W. G. Green was in August 1853 transferred to the 2nd Punjab Infantry as Commandant, when the following Regimental Order was issued :—

"Captain Vaughan, in the name of all ranks in the regiment, congratulates Lieutenant Green on the promotion which has fallen to him, but regrets at the same time that the regiment loses the services of an officer who has been associated with it from its first formation." *Lieutenant Green transferred to 2nd Punjab Infantry. Complimentary Order.*

Outpost of Viddore threatened. In September and October 1853 the outpost of Viddore was reinforced at a moment's notice to meet the threatened attacks of the Bozdars, &c.

Puckalies sanctioned. In October 1853 puckalies, one per company, were sanctioned in the room of hand bhistís. Each man was ordered to be supplied with a pair of leather bags ("pakkals") for carrying a supply of water on the march.

Target practice much improved. In November 1853 the following Regimental Order was issued :—

"The Commanding Officer, having kept a very careful record of each day's target practice during the last 18 months, is enabled to express his satisfaction at the improvement which has taken place since this time last year. On the 6th of November 1852 the number of hits per cent. at 100 yards was only 24. The last four days' practice at the same distance shows an average of 47¾ per cent."

Head-quarters march to Bannu. In December 1853 the head-quarters and the right wing of the regiment marched to Bannu in course of relief, the left wing taking its place temporarily at Dera Ghazi Khan.

Left wing joins head-quarters. In February 1854 the left wing rejoined head-quarters, and the regiment was united for the first time since April 1850.

Rifles for two companies received. Rifles (2-grooved) were received for two complete companies and issued to the flank companies. Consequent on this change in the arming of the regiment, the designation of Light and Grenadier Companies was discontinued and the companies were numbered from right to left.

Complimentary Order to Lieutenant Williamson. In March 1854 Lieutenant Williamson having been relieved of the duties of Adjutant, the following Regimental Order was published :—

"Lieutenant Williamson having, by the arrival of Lieutenant Lind, been relieved of the duties of Adjutant, which he has so zealously and efficiently performed for more than two years, the Officer Commanding desires to record his sense of Lieutenant Williamson's services in his late capacity. The temper, judgment and zeal which Lieutenant Williamson has invariably displayed are thoroughly appreciated by Captain Vaughan, who is glad to think that, though he loses Lieutenant Williamson's services as Adjutant, he retains them as 2nd-in-Command of the regiment."

Langris. Two "langrís" or cooks were added in March 1854 to the establishment of each company.

Turbans were substituted for the Kilmarnock caps hitherto worn.

Turbans.

In September 1854 two companies were ordered to Dera Ismail Khan to take the outpost duties of that frontier, and were so employed for four months.

Two companies detached to Dera Ismail Khan.

In November 1854 each man was provided with a Kabul "poshtín" at the cost of Rs. 2-2 to each non-commissioned officer and private, and Rs. 10 to each native officer.

Poshteens.

In March 1855 a company of the regiment was ordered to garrison Latumar whilst the Kohát force was employed in the Miranzai valley. The company was relieved on the 30th of May.

A company garrisons Latumar.

In June 1855 the composition was as follows :—

Composition of the regiment.

Hindustánís of all ranks	...	...	222
Sikhs and Punjubís ditto	...	...	548
Trans-Indus men ditto	...	...	157
	Total	...	927

In August 1855 the regiment was ordered to detach at a moment's notice three companies to garrison Latumar, Bahádur Khel and Nurri, in relief of the 3rd Punjab Infantry required to join a force assembled at Hangu. The order was received at 11 A.M., and the detachment marched at noon and reached Latumar, 19 miles, the same evening, and Bahádur Khel, 32 miles, without halting, at 11 P.M. One company marched onwards to Nurri next morning, and reached that place, 13 miles, some hours before noon. Subadár Mián Singh was in command. The detachment was relieved in October.

The rapid march of a detachment to Bahádur Khel and Nurri.

In April 1856 the regiment was inspected by Brigadier-General Neville Chamberlain, Commanding the Force.

Regiment inspected.

In August 1856, 25 recruits in excess of the establishment were authorized to be kept up on a subsistence allowance of Rs. 3 per mensem.

Twenty-five supernumerary recruits sanctioned.

In August 1856 a Native Adjutant was sanctioned, and Jemadár Gunga Dubi was appointed to the situation.

A Native Adjutant appointed.

In September 1856 rifles (2-grooved) for a third complete company were received and issued to No. 4 Company.

Rifles received for a third company.

The regiment furnishes the garrison of Latumar.

In September 1856 the outpost of Latumar having been transferred from the Kohát to the Bannu district, the garrison was furnished from the regiment.

Rapid march of a detachment to Bahádur Khel and Nurri.

In October 1856 a detachment of the regiment, 210 men of all ranks, marched to Bahádur Khel and Nurri to take the duties of those posts, consequent on the regiment being ordered to march to Kohát in course of relief.

Capture of smugglers' cattle.

Whilst in command of the detachment at Bahádur Khel, Subadár Sohan Tewary surprised a party of salt smugglers and captured all their cattle; the drovers would have been also caught but for the accidental discharge of a matchlock.

March of regiment to Kohát.

In October 1856 the head-quarters of the regiment marched to Kohát, and were followed a few days later by the remainder of the corps under Lieutenant Lind.

Two companies join the Miranzai Field Force.

In November 1856 Lieutenant Lind, with the 1st and 8th Companies of the regiment, proceeded to join the Miranzai Field Force under the command of Brigadier-General Chamberlain. Lieutenant Williamson remained in command at Kohát, the regiment being disposed of as follows :—

On outpost duties ...	... 210	of all ranks.
On field service ...	... 211	ditto.
In garrison at Kohát	... 507	ditto.

As many of the men in garrison at Kohát were sickly, and the guards and escorts furnished numerous, the duty during the absence of the Miranzai Field Force fell very heavily on the healthy men.

Lieutenant Lind's detachment rejoins.

In December 1856 Lieutenant Lind's detachment rejoined head-quarters on the breaking up of the Field Force. This detachment shared in Brigadier-General Chamberlain's complimentary order when the latter event took place.

Composition of the regiment.

In January 1857 the composition of the regiment was as follows :—

Hindustánís of all ranks		...	...	... 170
Cis-Sutlej men	ditto	...	...	... 78
Punjabís	ditto	...	...	... 470
Trans-Indus men	ditto	...	...	... 210
			Total	... 928

Of the above number 551 were Muhammadans, and the remaining 377 Sikhs and Hindús.

In February 1857 251 additional rifles were received and were issued to Nos. 2 and 7 Companies, and partially to No. 3. This made the number of 2-grooved rifles with the regiment up to 587.

More rifles received.

In bringing up the history of the regiment to this point (February 1857) it may be permitted to observe that, although during the seven years the regiment has been embodied, it has never had the good fortune to be actively engaged with an enemy, yet that it has borne a very large share of the duties of the Trans-Indus frontier, having at different times served at every station from Asnee to Kohát, and garrisoned every outpost on the whole line. The severity of the duty devolving upon the regiment when distributed between Dera Ghází Khán and Asnee in particular was such that in one year (1853) the furlough authorized for the force was obliged to be partially withheld, but under no circumstances has the smallest murmur been uttered, whilst the annals of the regiment will, it is believed, show a remarkable absence of crime generally.

Remarks on the nature of the services performed by the regiment up to the present time.

On the 13th March 1857 the head-quarters of the regiment, with the right wing and No. 8 Company, were warned to march on service towards Dera Ismail Khan on the 18th idem. The contemplated expedition against the powerful Wazíri tribe was, however, temporarily abandoned, and the order for the march countermanded.

Order to march to Dera Ismail Khan for service.

Regimental Order No. 188. dated 1st April 1857.

"It is with great regret Major Vaughan loses the services of Lieutenant Williamson, who has filled in turn, during the last five years, the several offices of Adjutant, 2nd-in-Command, and Officiating Commandant. Major Vaughan hopes the loss to the regiment will be only temporary, and assures Lieutenant Williamson of the pleasure that his return with renovated health will cause himself and all ranks."

Complimentary order to Lieutenant Williamson.

On the 1st May 1857 three companies were detached to take the duties of the outposts of Bahádur Khel and Nurri.

Three companies detached for outposts.

14th May 1857.—An express from Peshawar from Brigadier-General Chamberlain, Commanding the Force, was received at daybreak directing the regiment to march with the utmost expedition to Attock and secure that fortress, then

Ordered on service; march to Attock

held by a detachment of the 58th Bengal Native Infantry, which it was thought could not be trusted after the events which had taken place at Meerut and Delhi, and which had become partially known at Peshawar by the electric telegraph. The headquarters of the regiment marched the same night to Gumbat, Lieutenant Lind remaining behind to meet and bring on the three companies on duty at the outposts. It was thought advisable to adopt the route by Shádipore and the Nilabgarh, which had not hitherto been used by troops. The marches were very long and fatiguing, but the regiment reached Attock at about 8 A.M. on the 18th of May. The bridge of boats had been dismantled for the season the day before, but the headquarters and about 80 men crossed as rapidly as possible in boats, left a small guard in the Kabul gateway, and, pushing rapidly through the lower fort, occupied the Lahore Gate also. The garrison manifested great surprise at finding the Punjab soldiers arrived to relieve them ; but everything passed off quietly, and by 3 P.M. the fort was occupied at all points and the late garrison had been encamped outside, except half a company of Native Artillery, which was placed under strict surveillance.

Lieutenant Lind with a small party makes prisoners of a guard, 55th Native Infantry, and follows up a detachment of mutineers to Nowshera. On the 21st of May the detachment under Lieutenant Lind joined. That morning a loyal chief, Fatteh Khan, Khuttuck, who had been charged by the Commissioner of Peshawar with the duty of guarding the Khyrabad side of the ferry, reported to Major Vaughan certain mutinous language made use of to some of his followers by a guard of the 55th Native Infantry. Major Vaughan sent orders to Lieutenant Lind, as he was about to cross, to make this guard prisoners. The execution of this order seems to have alarmed a large party of the same regiment under a Native Officer on guard at the Engineer's timber yard ; instigated by the Native Officer, this party got under arms and marched towards Nowshera, threatening to fire on Lieutenant Lind, who endeavoured to dissuade them from committing such an open act of mutiny. Except about 12 men, all of Lieutenant Lind's detachment had by this time crossed the river, but with this small party he followed the mutineers (from 30 to 40 in number), and though not strong enough to attack them, he made two prisoners, and by alarming the police posts along the road got information of what was happening conveyed to Nowshera in time to prepare the Officer Commanding that station for the arrival of the mutineers.

On this occasion Lieutenant Lind reported very favourably of the conduct of Havildár Muddeh Khan, and of Privates Gordut Singh and Mir Ahmed Khan.

On the evening of the 21st of May instructions were received from Sir John Lawrence to raise immediately four additional companies.

Order to raise four additional companies.

On the 22nd May 1857 an express from the Brigadier Commanding reached the Commanding Officer at 2 P.M. directing the regiment to march immediately to Nowshera and to attack, if necessary, a portion of the 55th Native Infantry, said to have broken out into flagrant mutiny. Accordingly, in the dusk of the evening, the regiment crossed the Indus with some difficulty in consequence of a violent gale of wind, and marching all night reached Nowshera at daylight, when it was ascertained that the mutineers had returned to their duty to some extent and had been marched to Mardán to rejoin the head-quarters of their regiment. The regiment was then placed in temporary quarters in the British barracks, so as to protect the families of Her Majesty's 27th Regiment in the event of any rise on the part of the other Native Regiment (the 10th Irregular Cavalry) at the station.

March to Nowshera.

On the morning of the 24th of May 1857 the following despatch was received from the Commissioner of Peshawar :—

March to Mardán and the attack and pursuit of the mutinous 55th Native Infantry.

From Lieutenant-Colonel EDWARDES, C.B., to Major J. L. VAUGHAN, Commanding 5th Punjab Infantry, dated Peshawar, 10 P.M., 23rd May 1857.

" By desire of Brigadier Sydney Cotton, Commanding Peshawar Division, I have the honor to acquaint you that, an hour hence, a small force of 300 European Infantry and about 250 Cavalry (Native Irregulars) and 8 guns, 6 of which are howitzers, will march from this cantonment to the ferry of Dobundi, and thence proceed tomorrow night in one long march to the Fort of Mardán for the purpose of disarming the 55th Native Infantry, which is said to be in a state of mutiny.

" 2. The Brigadier desires that (unless circumstances at Nowshera, of which you alone can judge, render it impracticable or inexpedient) you will co-operate with the above force by sending 200 men of your regiment, or as nearly that number as you can manage, fully equipped for service, to join the Peshawur Column on its line of march on the

morning of the 25th of May between Doseyree and Mardán, so as to
effect the junction a few miles before reaching the scene of action, and
run no risk of your encountering the mutinous regiment single-handed.

"3. A suitable point will probably be in the neighbourhood of
Koorgh Deyri, to the westward of Mardán (see Walker's map).

"4. The Peshawar Column is directed to arrive at Mardán before
gunfire on the morning of the 25th May.

"5. It is just possible that the mutineers may break from the
Fort of Mardán and make for the Fort of Abazai to join the detachment
of the 64th Native Infantry there; and you will endeavour, of course,
during the day and night of 24th May, to obtain reliable information of
the position of the 55th Native Infantry, and communicate as quickly
as you can to the Peshawar Column any move that may come to your
knowledge."

Agreeably to the foregoing instructions the head-quarters
left Nowshera barracks at 4 P.M. on the 24th May and reached
the rendezvous at Koorgh Deyri about an hour before daybreak on the 25th, but circumstances had delayed the Peshawar
Column, and the whole force was not united until after sunrise.
In the meantime the 55th Native Infantry had abandoned the
Fort of Mardán and were marching towards the Swát Hills. As
soon as this was known, the regiment, with all the cavalry
and artillery, was sent in pursuit.

This most harassing duty was performed with excellent
spirit, and the pursuit was continued as far as Jamál Garhi,
7 miles from Mardán, many of the enemy's stragglers being
shot or bayoneted. At Jamál Garhi it was found absolutely
necessary to halt for a short time to refresh the men, who had
then been marching for 22 hours. At 4 P.M. the regiment
was formed up to continue the pursuit, but had hardly set forward when it was halted by Lieutenant-Colonel J. Nicholson,
who had made, what he considered, adequate arrangements to
prevent the mutineers from leaving a high mountain on which
they had taken refuge, until the regiment and two mountain
train guns should be in a position to attack them next morning.
Accordingly the regiment bivouacked for the night at Jamál
Garhi, and at daylight again set forward in the hope of coming
up with the mutineers, but on reaching the village of Multah
it was found that the latter had effected their escape
during the night and had succeeded in crossing the British

border. It was not thought advisable to harass the men further, and the regiment was therefore ordered back to Mardán; but Major Vaughan, with a few horsemen (including Subadár Habíb Khan, 9th Company), pushed on by the road the mutineers had taken and ascertained their movements with certainty.

Extract from Major Vaughan's report of the above affair :—

"I have to report that I received every assistance from my 2nd-in-Command, Lieutenant Lind, and that I am in every way satisfied with the conduct of my men, who went through great fatigue with zeal and cheerfulness, and were always anxious to push on."

Regimental Order, dated Camp Mardán, 26th May 1857.

"In obedience to Field Force Order of to-day, the regiment will furnish a firing party of six files under a non-commissioned officer for the execution of the mutineers condemned to death by Drum-Head Court-Martial this afternoon." *The regiment furnishes a firing party to execute mutineers.*

27th May 1857.—The regiment was now attached to the Peshawar Column, which it was thought advisable should be encamped for a time in the neighbourhood of Fort Abazai on the Swát river, to watch the movements of a noted outlaw named ___, a refugee in Swát, who designed at this time to enter the Pesháwar Valley at the head of a considerable following and to kindle a religious war. The column accordingly marched from Mardán on the night of the 27th May, and reached Abazai in three marches. Neither the officers or men had their tents with them, the camp having been left standing at Attock on the 22nd of May; but the inconvenience was cheerfully borne, and it was alleviated as much as possible by the kindness of Colonel Chute, Commanding the Force, who made over all the spare tents attached to the column for the use of the regiment. *The regiment is attached to the Peshawar Moveable Column.*

Extract from Field Force Orders by Colonel Chute, Commanding :— *Ordered to Mardán.*

Dated Camp Utmanzai, 12th June 1857.

"Agreeably to instructions received from Divisional Head-Quarters, the 5th Punjab Infantry, as also two mountain train howitzers, under the command of a European officer, to be detailed by Major Barr, Commanding the Artillery, the whole to be under the command of Major Vaughan, will proceed from Nisultah on the 14th instant to Hoti Mardán, there to be stationed. *Complimentary Order.*

" Colonel Chute, Commanding the Field Force, cannot permit the 5th
Punjab Infantry to leave the force under his command without expressing his best thanks to Major Vaughan and the officers and men of his
regiment for their valuable services at Hoti Mardán on the 25th ultimo,
as also for their excellent conduct while under his command in camp
and quarters."

Regimental Order, dated Camp Mardán, 16th June 1857.

**Occupies the
Fort of Mar-
dan.**
" The regiment will move into the fort and take up
quarters, which will be pointed out to Native Officers of companies.

" On the arrival at Nowshera of Lieutenant W. D. Hoste, 55th
Native Infantry, who has been appointed to do duty with the regiment,
Lieutenant and Adjutant Forbes will be pleased to make over to him the
command of the Attock and Nowshera detachments, and will rejoin
Regimental Head-Quarters."

**Rifles (2-
grooved)
received for
the four
additional
companies.**
17th June 1857.—Major Vaughan reported, for the information of the Brigadier Commanding, that he had received from
the Peshawar Magazine enough rifles to equip the four additional companies of the regiment with that arm.

**Memo. of dis-
tribution of
regiment.**
25th June 1857.—Memo. of effective strength and distribution of the regiment on this date :—

At Head-Quarters	...	312 rifles.
At Nowshera	...	90 ,,
At Attock	...	98 ,,

The remainder of the regiment was on furlough, except
a few men on command and escort. There were also 131
recruits.

**Transfer of
men to 18th
Punjab In-
fantry.**
30th June 1857.—One Subadár, 1 Jemadár, 4 Havildárs,
8 Naicks and 50 Privates were transferred to Captain Bartlett's
Irregular Levy at Peshawar (now 18th Punjab Infantry).

**Political con-
dition of Eu-
safzai.**
A few words explanatory of the political condition of
the country in which the regiment was located will not be
out of place. For many years Eusafzai had been controlled
by the Guide Corps, which was permanently quartered at Fort
Mardán. The Guides had, about the middle of May 1857,
been withdrawn for service in Hindustán, and their
place had been temporarily supplied by the 55th Native
Infantry. The mutiny of the latter corps had been promptly

visited, and a severe loss inflicted upon the mutineers, but still the fact that nearly 700 armed soldiers in open revolt against the Government had contrived to cross the frontier unharmed and were seeking, or had obtained, service with an independent tribe beyond the border, combined with the events then passing in Hindustán, could not fail to have a bad effect upon the minds of the warlike and only lately-tamed Eusafzais. The danger was heightened by the circumstance that a revolution had occurred about this time in Swát, which led to the ex-king, with a considerable following, seeking an asylum in Punjtar (which is only separated from Eusafzai by a low range of hills), and there entering into correspondence with the heads of the colonies of fanatical Hindustánís at Sittána and Mangaltána, who again were in close coalition with the rebels at Delhi and elsewhere. It was therefore to be expected that attempts would be made to excite the Eusafzais to rebellion, and to adopt so favourable an opportunity of regaining that species of barbarous independence which they had lost under British rule. The first symptom of the success of such an intrigue was soon visible.

2nd July 1857.—Copy of a report addressed by Major Vaughan, Commanding 5th Punjab Infantry, to the Assistant Adjutant-General at Pesháwar :—

Attack on Shaikh Jana. Spin Khana and Gangu Dair.

" I have the honor to report, for the information of the Brigadier-General Commanding, the Pesháwar Division, that, at the requisition of Lieutenant Horne, Assistant Commissioner of Eusafzai, I moved out of Mardán at 4 P.M. yesterday with the force as per margin in view to act, as circumstances might require, against certain Eusafzai villages on the Khodukhel and Punjtar border, reported to be in a state of revolt against the Government.

Two guns. Peshawar Mountain Train.
Eighty sabres, 2nd Punjab Cavalry.
Two hundred and seventy rifles, 5th Punjab Infantry.

The force bivouacked during the night at the village of Sher Gund, about 18 miles east of Mardán. Intelligence arrived during the night that parties of horsemen from beyond the border were in the villages of Shaikh Jána and Sota and that the inhabitants of both these villages and of Gangu Dair were aiding and abetting these horsemen in their hostile designs against the Government. With Lieutenant Horne's entire concurrence, I determined to attack the large village of Shaikh Jána at daybreak. We found a considerable number of horsemen and matchlockmen drawn up along the eastern bank of the nullah upon which Shaikh Jána is built. Three or four rounds from the guns put them speedily into disorder. The skirmishers of the 5th Punjab Infantry then cleared the village, and the cavalry pursued the fugitives over the open plain in its rear, driving them into the adjoining village of Spín Khána. I immediately re-formed and attacked Spín Khána. A single round from the guns again put the defenders into disorder, the infantry pushed on through the village, and the cavalry pursued the enemy as they iguominiously fled to the hills in the direction of Bágh, cutting up several, and making about 25 prisoners, amongst others a well-known character on this border, named Ján Muhammad. The village of Gangu Dair was found deserted. I propose to destroy it, as well as Shaikh Jána and Spín Khána. The troops behaved admirably, and the pursuit of the fugitives by the detachment, 2nd Punjab Cavalry, under Lieutenant Graham was conducted in the most spirited manner.

"As it will assist the collection of the revenue, I propose to remain for a few days in the neighbourhood with the force.

"Our only casualties were two troopers, 2nd Punjab Cavalry, severely wounded."

Regiment returns to Mardan.

10th July 1857.—The regiment returned to Mardán.

Narinji.

The effect of the prompt punishment which had befallen the Shaikh Jána insurgents was complete as far as the population of the open country was concerned, but an emissary from the Hindustáni colonists, before alluded to, in the person of one Maulvi Ináyat Ali, repaired to the strong mountain village of Narinjí about a fortnight later, and there raised the standard of religious war. Narinjí is on the extreme border, and, being very difficult of access, had become an asylum for bad characters, and had several times defied the authorities in Eusafzai. At the last moment, however, the Maliks had always saved the place from destruction by timely submission and reparation. Their present reception of the invading Maulvi was a challenge to us to fight it out.

Report of first attack on Narinji.

21st July 1857.—Copy of a report addressed by Major Vaughan, Commanding 5th Punjab Infantry, to the Assistant Adjutant-General at Pesháwar :—

"The Brigadier-General Commanding the Pesháwar Division will doubtless have been made aware of the circumstances which have led the Civil authorities of Pesháwar to determine to punish the large Eusafzai frontier village of Narinjí, situated 23 miles north-east of Mardán, so I shall confine myself to relating the proceedings of the force placed at my disposal for this purpose.

"2. Three hundred rifles of the 4th Punjab Infantry having reached Mardán from N:wshera on the 18th, a field force as per margin marched that night to Yar Hussain, 13 miles east of Mardán. The route taken was intended to mislead the Narinjí people, and to indicate an intention of proceeding against the Punjtar Chief, and this idea was confirmed by Captain James having ordered supplies for a force to be prepared at another village on the Punjtar side. The 4th Punjab Infantry had arrived so late on the 18th instant at Mardán, owing to the difficulty of crossing the Kabul river, that I was obliged to halt on the 20th to refresh them.

Margin: Four mountain train guns. One troop, 2nd Punjab Cavalry. Three hundred rifles, 4th Punjab Infantry. Four hundred rifles, 5th Punjab Infantry.

"Captain Wilde, the Commandant, and a number of men (30) were attacked by heat apoplexy from the effects of this exposure and their services lost to the force.

"3. On the night of the 20th I marched to Narinjí, 13 miles. The arrival of the force was quite unexpected, and the surprise complete.

"4. I found the position of the village to be very strong. It is built in terraces at the foot of a lofty mountain, which embraces it on three sides, and the slope of which, though practicable for infantry, is very steep. A broad sandy nullah runs along the foot of this mountain, and on the other side of this nullah, facing Narinjí, is another range of heights, also of considerable altitude.

"5. With a sufficient force of infantry I should have attempted to crown the heights above the village before attacking the village in front, but with less than 700 infantry, already fatigued by a long night march at this season of the year, I judged it unadvisable, whilst the enemy's strength was undeveloped, to divide my force and attempt the long and laborious operation of crowning the mountain, the paths of which were quite unknown to the guides. I therefore took up a position to throw shot and shell into the village from the mountain train guns (two 3-pounder guns and two 2-pounder howitzers), trusting thus to do it some mischief, and partially clear it of the enemy, before employing the infantry to fire the houses and destroy the stores of grain they contained.

"6. After some rounds from the guns, the infantry accordingly advanced against the village in skirmishing order, and after a tenacious resistance made themselves masters of all but a few of the uppermost houses. The enemy, who were very numerous, behaved with great bravery, and constantly attacked sword in hand, and, when driven out of the village, took their post on the mountain above it, and maintained a desultory fire upon the troops, whose efforts to destroy the village were thus materially impeded. However, all the lower buildings were eventually fired, and as much mischief done as under the circumstances was possible.

" 7.   The success of the attack must be judged more by the loss in
men inflicted on the enemy than by the injury done to the village.   I
believe this affair will challenge comparison in this respect with any
similar affair which has taken place on this border.   Independent
of those who must have been killed by the guns (which fired 35
rounds each before and during the infantry attack) on the higher
slopes above the village, which the infantry did not reach, fifty
of the enemy fell within the lower part of the village alone.   Many of
these were Purbiás, probably stragglers from the late 55th Native
Infantry.   The wounded may be calculated at, at least, fifty more.

" 8.   At 8 A.M. I recalled the troops, believing that all that our
means admitted had been achieved.   I knew that the troops were
much exhausted by their long night march and four hours of fighting.
The supply of water was uncertain, the greater part of that available
for the troops having been brought from the villages in the rear by
Captain James's excellent arrangements. Above all, men began to appear
on the heights above Narinjí, and on our flank and rear, which led me to
expect that our retreat, whenever made, would be vigorously opposed.

" 9.   That the enemy were dispirited to no ordinary extent by the
loss we had inflicted upon them may, I think, be gathered from the
unprecedented fact that our retreat was conducted without the
smallest opposition from the enemy, who, though the ground was
most favourable, did not fire a single shot throughout the operation
of withdrawing the troops.

" 10.   Captain Browne with the troop of the 2nd Punjab Cavalry
made a most spirited charge after a party carrying off cattle, and
captured more than 100 head.   The mounted police under Captain
James were also most useful, and cut up several of the enemy, who on
one occasion ventured down into the bed of the nullah.

" 11.   I am much indebted to all the European officers with the
force, military and medical, and the conduct of the troops of all
arms was excellent throughout.

" 12.   I am also much indebted to Captain James for the excellence
of all his arrangements and for the assistance he rendered me throughout.

" 13.   I append a return of casualties.

Casualty List.

Detachment, Peshawar Mountain Train—wounded, 1 mule.

Detachment, 2nd Punjab Cavalry—killed, 1 horse.

4th Punjab Infantry—killed, 1 Naick, 2 privates; wounded,
  1 Havildár, 2 Naicks and 5 privates.

5th Punjab Infantry—killed, 2 privates ; wounded, 1 Jemadár,
  1 bugler and 11 privates.

Total killed, 1 Naick and 4 privates, 1 horse; wounded, 1 Jemadár,
  1 Havildár, 1 Naick, 1 bugler, 16 privates, 1 mule.

"*P.S.*—To show the trying nature of the weather, forty men soldiers and followers, were struck down by the sun, of whom nine have died, including the Farrier Sergeant of the Peshawar Mountain Train."

KILLED IN V. P. I.

Sepoy Ghafúr Khan. | Sepoy Shádah.

WOUNDED IN V. P. I.

Jemadár Karam Khan.	Sepoy Sharfah.
Bugler Sikandar.	„ Jiwah.
Sepoy Sáwan.	„ Bahádur Shah.
„ Phúla Singh.	„ Abdul Azíz.
„ Badháwah Singh.	„ Fateh.
„ Nathu.	„ Mozah Khan.
„ Jowáya.	

1st August 1857.—The regiment was encamped in the neighbourhood of the large village of Shewa after the affair of the 21st July, until it should be seen if any further operations against Maulvi Ináyat Ali and his adherents at Narinjí would be necessary. It was decided that the village should be re-attacked and totally destroyed, and this was successfully accomplished on the 3rd of August, as shown in the following report :—

Second attack on Narinjí.

From Major J. L. VAUGHAN, Commanding 5th Punjab Infantry, to the Assistant Adjutant-General at Peshawar,—dated Camp Shewa, Yusafzai, 3rd August 1857.

I have the honor to report for the information of Brigadier-General Cotton, Commanding the Peshawar Division, the successful conclusion of the operations against the village of Narinjí.

"2. Having yesterday received the reinforcements sent by the Brigadier-General as per margin, I made all arrangements for re-attacking and entirely destroying Narinjí this morning, as follows.

2 24-pounder howitzers.
50 H. M.'s 27th Foot,
50 H. M.'s 87th Foot.
50 H. M.'s 70th Foot.
50 21st Regiment Native Infantry.
200 6th Punjab Infantry.
150 Captain Cave's regiment.
100 Horse Levies.
140 Foot Levies.

"3. A column consisting of 300 rifles of the 5th Punjab Infantry and 50 men of Her Majesty's 27th Regiment, the whole commanded by Lieutenant Hoste of the former corps, left the line of march about 1½ miles from Narinjí, with orders to ascend the hills at a given point and appear in rear of and above the village, which the rest of the troops would in the meanwhile attack in front.

"4. As soon as the main column arrived opposite the village, fire was opened upon it, and upon the clusters of men observed upon different points of the mountain, from the 24-pounder howitzers and the mountain train guns. This was feebly replied to by a matchlock fire from the Sungahs, &c., above the village and along the heights.

" 5. After this had continued about half an hour, the column which had been detached to ascend the hill made its appearance far away on the right. Its progress was vigorously opposed by the enemy, but the latter were dislodged from every point where they attempted to stand, and the column pushed on in the most brilliant manner and without a check until the rear of the village was gained. The upper portion of the village, which is very strong and commanding, and other points overlooking the village, were then rapidly taken possession of at the point of the bayonet by a portion of Lieutenant Hoste's men, whilst the remainder continued their advance in pursuit of the enemy until the heights westward of the village were also cleared.

" 6. After the success of Lieutenant Hoste's column was no longer doubtful, I sent the detachment, 6th Punjab Infantry, under Lieutenant Saunders, to ascend the heights which inclose the village to the westward, and intercept the retreat of the fugitives. This service was well performed, and 25 or 30 of the enemy were killed. Amongst the slain were several Purbiás, believed from their arms and accoutrements to be men of the late 55th Native Infantry.

" 7. Simultaneously with the movement last described, Captain Cave's men and 50 of Her Majesty's 70th Regiment entered the village from the front and found it deserted.

" 8. The work of destruction then commenced : not a house was spared, even the walls of many were destroyed by the aid of elephants. The village was soon a mass of ruins.

" 9. When everything was completed the troops were withdrawn. Not a shot had been fired at us during the six hours we held possession of the village, nor was a shot fired on us as we withdrew.

" 10. The Brigadier-General may be assured that the whole operation was perfectly successful, whilst our casualties were few. The loss of the enemy was from 30 to 35 killed ; of the wounded I have as yet no accounts.

" 11. Though not actively engaged, the large force of cavalry at disposal gave great security of movement to the guns and infantry in the bed of the nullah.

" 12. Some of the foot levies were very useful in occupying the heights in our rear opposite the village, from which I had anticipated possible annoyance."

Casualties.

Killed, Detachment 6th Punjab Infantry		1 private.
Wounded, 5th Punjab Infantry	...	5 privates.
Do., 6th Punjab Infantry	...	1 private.
Do., Captain Cave's regiment	...	2 privates.

Names of men of the 5th Punjab Infantry who were wounded :—

Sepoy Ahmudjee.

   „ Roudah.

   „ Sher Khan.

   „ ——— -

   „ ———

6th August 1857.—The regiment returned into quarters at Mardán. *Regiment returns to Mardan.*

7th August 1857.—The four additional companies ordered to be raised on the 21st of May were struck off the rolls and ordered to join the 8th Punjab Infantry at Nowshera. *The four additional companies transferred to 8th Punjab Infantry.*

8th August 1857.—The original eight companies of which the regiment was composed were divided into ten. *The regiment re-distributed into ten companies.*

20th August 1857.—Extract of a letter from the Military Secretary to the Chief Commissioner, dated Lahore, 17th August 1857 :— *Turbans presented in the name of the Chief Commissioner to two Native Officers.*

" With reference to your demi-official letter to the Staff Officer, Punjab Frontier Force, dated the 9th instant, requesting the Chief Commissioner to bestow pugries on Subadár Lál Khan and Jemadár Aziz Khan (for their gallant conduct in action at Narinjí on the 3rd of August), I am instructed by the Chief Commissioner to request you will be good enough to purchase two handsome loougies and present them to the Native Officers in his name."

31st December 1857.—The regiment being about to proceed to Hindustán on service, the Chief Commissioner directed the entertainment of 100 supernumerary recruits. *One hundred supernumerary recruits ordered to be entertained.*

3rd January 1858.—The regiment commenced its march towards Hindustán. *The regiment marches down-country.*

Extract from letter No. 255, from the Deputy Assistant Quartermaster-General, to the Officer Commanding 5th Punjab Infantry, dated Camp Cawnpore, 4th February 1858 :— *The Commander-in-Chief expresses approval of the rapid progress made by the regiment down-country.*

" His Excellency the Commander-in-Chief desires me to convey to you his approval of the rapid progress you are making with your regiment down-country."

14th February 1858.—The regiment reached Meerut, and was halted by order of Major-General Penny, c.b., Commanding the Meerut Division. *Reaches and halts at Meerut.*

7th March 1858.—The regiment marched towards Allygurh and Khasgunge with a force under Major-General Penny, c.b. *Marches towards Allygurh.*

Marches towards Lucknow.   19*th March* 1858.—Under Army Head-Quarters' orders the regiment was directed to march forthwith towards Lucknow.

Arrives at Lucknow.   2*nd April* 1858.—The regiment arrived at Lucknow.

Six companies joined Sir Hope Grant's field force.   9*th April* 1858.—The head-quarters of the regiment with six companies were attached to a field force under Major-General Sir Hope Grant, K.C B., and marched on the 11th April towards Seetapore.

Action at Baree.   13*th April* 1858.—Sir Hope Grant's force expelled a considerable body of rebels under the Lucknow Maulvi this day from the neighbourhood of Baree, but the Infantry Brigade (Her Majesty's 38th, 2nd Battalion, Rifle Brigade, 1st Bengal Fusiliers and 5th Punjab Infantry) were but very slightly engaged. The force, after making a circuit by Mahomedabad, Ramnuggar and Nawábgunge, returned to Lucknow on the 27th of April. On the 28th, the 90th Light Infantry having been substituted for the 1st Bengal Fusiliers in the Infantry Brigade, the force marched towards the *Action of Simree.* Biswárn district of Oudh, where the rebels mustered in great force under Bance Madho. No engagement, however, took place until the 13th of May, on which day the force moved from its camp at Nugger at 3 P.M. to attack a large body of rebels in the jungle about Simree. The left being threatened by the rebels, Nos. 9 and 10 Companies, and subsequently the whole of the regiment and the brigade, made a change of front and advanced. The advance was covered by Nos. 9 and 10 Companies in skirmishing order, and these companies came upon a large body of rebels protected by the banks of a deep nullah, and attacked them in a most spirited way and with perfect success, killing a considerable number and causing the hurried retreat of the remainder before the supports could come into action. No. 9, a very young company, composed entirely of Patháns, particularly distinguished itself on this occasion, and lost one private killed, and a Native Officer and seven privates wounded :—

Killed—Sepoy Sáhib Alam.
Wounded—Jemadár Rehmán Khan.
       Sepoy Joomah Khan.
       „ Mohamed Khan.
       „ Akber.
       „ Abdool Mohamed.
       „ Ali Gool.
       „ Manah Singh.
       „ Jowáhir Singh.

13*th June* 1858.—Extract from Regimental Order No.
234 :—

" The Commanding Officer considers it just to place upon record his
approval of the behaviour of the regiment in action with the enemy
this morning, when it was brought for the first time under the
fire of artillery. The advance of the regiment in light infantry
order against a body of the enemy's infantry and two guns was executed
with a firmness and spirit which ensured success."

June and July 1858.—The regiment and other troops
were ordered to hut themselves for the rains at Nawábgunge.
The ground was prepared, and the materials cut and collected
by the men themselves; it was only in thatching the huts that
the labour of artisans was employed.

Regimental Order No. 304, dated 21st July 1858.

F. Troop, Royal Horse
Artillery.
Field Battery, Royal
Artillery.
7th Hussars.
2nd Battalion, Rifle Bri-
gade.
1st Madras Fusiliers.
5th Punjab Infantry.

" The troops noted in the margin being
ordered to march to Fyzabad by Division
Order No. 1 of this date, the regiment will
be formed in column of march, &c."

The regi-
ment
marches
with the
field force
towards
Fyzabad.

Regimental Order No. 305, dated 22nd July 1858.

F. Troop, Royal Horse
Artillery.
200 men, 7th Hussars.
200 men, Hodson's Horse.

" The regiment will march, together with
the troops noted in the margin, on a particular service at 11 P.M."

Regimental Order No. 306, dated 23rd July 1858.

" The Commanding Officer is well pleased with the manner in
which the very fatiguing march of last night was performed, and with
the patience and spirit displayed in supporting the cavalry over very
heavy ground this morning, after having been twelve hours under arms,
the latter part of the time under a burning sun. It is matter of regret
that the precipitate retreat of the enemy prevented the regiment from
closing with them."

Fyzabad was re-occupied by the force under Major-General
Sir Hope Grant on the 29th July without opposition on
the part of the rebels. It was then determined to drive the
rebels out of Sultánpore also.

Regimental Order No. 324, dated 4th August 1858.

F. Troop, Royal Horse
Artillery.
7th Hussars.
250 Sabres Hodson's Horse.
1st Madras Fusiliers.
5th Punjab Infantry.

" The force named in the margin having
by Division Order of this date been warned
to proceed towards Sultánpore on the morning
of the 6th instant, the regiment will be held
in readiness accordingly."

11th August 1858.—The force having arrived in the neighbourhood of Sultánpore on the left bank of the Goomtee, camp was formed, and the 5th Punjab Infantry was sent forward with two Horse Artillery guns to reconnoitre and occu-

py the town. In the course of this service it was discovered that a large body of the enemy (who were supposed to hold the Cantonment of Sultánpore on the right bank of the Goomtee) had crossed to the left bank. They were immediately attacked under the personal direction of Brigadier Horsford, Commanding the Force, and driven across the river, whereupon their guns opened upon the regiment, and a heavy fire of musketry levelled at No. 1 Company which in skirmishing order had then reached the river bank. The fire of the two Horse Artillery guns sufficed to check the enemy's artillery, and the musketry fire was gradually overcome by the rifles of the regiment, as other companies were pushed up to the support of No. 1 Company. The duty of guarding the river bank from any attempt of the enemy to re-cross was then assigned to the regiment, supported by the two Horse Artillery guns, and camp was formed close to the town of Sultánpore, about 1,200 yards from the Cantonment. In the course of the afternoon, however, it became necessary, in consequence of the enemy having re-opened fire from several guns at different points, to issue the following order :—

"Officers of companies are directed to march their companies from the present camp (leaving their tents standing) and get their men under cover in the town from the enemy's shot."

The amount of work which devolved upon the regiment during the succeeding fortnight was very considerable. It was necessary that one company should night and day hold the river bank opposite the Cantonments to repel any attempt to cross. As this company was so extended along the bank, each man sheltering himself from the fire from the houses, &c., opposite, as best he could, it was necessary to relieve it morning and evening that the men might get their meals, and as the monsoon was at its height, the men of the company were almost constantly wet. Another company was constantly on duty as a guard to the artillery picket of two Horse Artillery guns, and other points of the river, extending in all over a length of at least six miles, had to be watched by pickets, which were constantly under fire from the enemy. It was, however, initiation into the duties of a rifle regiment on service, and all ranks benefited by the practical lesson in outpost duties and skirmishing which they here received. In the meanwhile reinforcements were pushed up from Fyzabad by Sir Hope Grant, who arrived in person about the 22nd of August, and the Engineers were busily employed in preparing rafts, a work of difficulty, as all the boats on the Goomtee had been previously secured by the enemy.

Regimental Order No. 365, dated 26th August 1858.

" The force noted in the margin having driven the outposts of the enemy from their position on the right bank of the Goomtee, the regiment will encamp on the left of the Madras Fusiliers."

2 Guns, Royal Artillery.
1st Madras Fusiliers.
5th Punjab Infantry.

Enemy's outposts driven in.

Regimental Order No. 369, dated Right bank of Goomtee, 28th August 1858.

" The Commanding Officer records with much approval the spirited behaviour of No. 3 Company (the inlying picket) this morning in driving back, led by Captain W. D. Hoste and Lieutenant Stewart, a strong party of the enemy's infantry which was threatening the camp. The considerable punishment inflicted upon the enemy without loss on our side evinces the excellence of Captain Hoste's arrangements, and entitles that officer, as well as all concerned, to the Commanding Officer's best acknowledgments."

The spirited behaviour of No. 3 Company.

Regimental Order No. 372, dated Camp Sultánpore Contonment, 29th August 1858.

" The conduct of the regiment in driving the enemy yesterday evening from the neighbourhood of camp was everything the Commanding Officer could have wished, and the men were at the same time eager, steady, and obedient. The latter qualities were conspicuous in the way in which the delicate operation of covering the retirement of the whole force to camp after nightfall was performed. In placing the above on record, the Commanding Officer begs that the two European officers with the regiment, Captain W. D. Hoste, 2nd-in-Command, and Lieutenant C. E. Stewart, Adjutant, will accept his best thanks for their valuable services."

Enemy's attack repulsed. The regiment covers the retirement of the force to camp.

Regimental Order No. 373, dated Camp Sultánpore Contonment, 29th August 1858.

" The operations in which the regiment has been engaged since the 13th instant having been brought to a close by the retreat of the enemy from the neighbourhood of Sultánpore, the Commanding Officers desires to acknowledge the excellent behaviour of all ranks during the period in question. A large amount of harassing duty has been performed by the regiment, and in a cheerful and soldier-like manner, and Major-General Sir Hope Grant, Commanding, has assured Major Vaughan that the services rendered by the regiment in expediting the crossing of the river by so large a force have his warmest approval."

Regimental Order on the conclusion of operations.

Extract from
Sir Hope
Grant's des-
patch.

Extract from Major-General Sir Hope Grant's despatch relating to the foregoing operations, published in G. O. C. C., dated 9th November 1858 :—

" All Officers, Non-Commissioned Officers and men of this column have performed their various duties cheerfully and well, and deserve my full approval. I have particularly to notice the great assistance rendered by the Punjab Rifles, and Major Daly's corps in swimming across the Artillery and 7th Hussars' horses."

Casualties.

The regiment had three men wounded in the above operations from the 22nd to the 30th August 1858 :—

Sepoy Prem Singh.

„   Rám Kishan.

„   —————

Force goes
into stand-
ing camp.

The greater portion of the force under Sir Hope Grant went into standing camp after the occupation of Sultánpore Cantonments. and the regiment was quartered in and adjoining the houses of the Sadar Bazár.

Two compa-
nies detached
under Cap-
tain Hoste.

On the 6th of September 1858 the 4th and 5th Companies under Captain Hoste's command were attached to a force as per margin, which took up a position at Burtipore and Sailkah on the Fyzabad road in furtherance of the general plan of the campaign.

2 Horse Artillery guns.
100 Sabres, Hodson's Horse.
200, 53rd Regiment.
100, 5th Punjab Infantry.

Regimental Order No. 428, dated Sultánpore, 28th September 1858.

Regiment
inspected by
Brigadier
Horsford

" Major Vaughan has been desired by Brigadier Horsford, c.b., to explain to the regiment that he was very much pleased with the manner in which the regiment exercised this morning at inspection, and, further, that he accords the regiment high praise for its excellent behaviour in all respects during the six months that it has been under his command."

Three com-
panies de-
tached
under Lieut.
C. E.
Stewart.

On the 6th October 1858 the 6th, 7th and 8th Companies, under command of Lieutenant and Adjutant C. E. Stewart, were attached to a force as per margin, which marched to beat up some rebel bodies to the eastward in the direction of the Tonse nullah and the Azimgarh frontier.

2, Horse Artillery guns.
50, 7th Hussars.
25, Hodson's Horse.
200, Madras Fusiliers.
280, 5th Regiment P. I.

On the 10th of October 1858 the head-quarters of the regiment and force as per margin marched under Sir Hope Grant's personal command in view to expelling the rebels entirely from the eastern portion of Oudh previous to an advance against the forts of Amethee and Sunkurpore, Banee Mádho Singh's stronghold.

1 18-pounder gun.
1 8-inch howitzer.
4 Mortars.
2 Horse Artillery guns.
3 Troops, 7th Hussars.
75 Hodson's Horse.
2nd Battalion, Rifle Brigade.

Regimental head-quarters march with a force under command of Sir Hope Grant.

Regimental Order, dated Camp Dostpore, 17th October 1858.

" The Commanding Officer having received a report from Captain Hoste, 2nd-in-Command, of very gallant behaviour on the part of Havildár Mouzah Khan, Naick Báz Gul, and Privates Fazul Khan and Madee, all of the 4th Company, is pleased to reward them as follows— Havildár Mouzah Khan to be a Color Havildár, Naick Báz Gul to be a Havildár. Privates Fazul Khan and Madee to be Lance Naicks, the whole of the above with effect from the 15th instant."

Gallant behaviour of Non-Commissioned Officers and Privates of No. 4 Company.

Regimental Order, dated Camp Jasingpore, 22nd October 1858.

" Major Vaughan has received with much gratification a report from Captain W. D. Hoste, 2nd-in-Command, relating to the share borne by a detachment of the regiment under his command in an affair with the enemy in the neighbourhood of Sultánpore on the 20th instant, in which guns, ammunition, elephants, &c., were captured by a force under the command of Brigadier Horsford, c.b. Captain Hoste has added another to the many obligations Major Vaughan already owes him for his conduct on similar occasions, and the detachment under Captain Hoste's orders has well sustained the reputation of the regiment and of the Punjab Irregular Force. Major Vaughan begs Captain Hoste to accept his warm congratulations, and convey them also to the whole of his detachment."

Affair near Sultanpore in which Captain Hoste's detachment was engaged.

24th October 1858.—The whole of the regiment was reunited this day at Sultánpore by the return of the head-quarters to that place and the junction of Captain Hoste's and Lieutenant Stewart's detachments.

The regiment is re-united.

Regimental Order No. 455, dated 24th October 1858.

" The Commanding Officer has received a report from Lieutenant and Adjutant C. E. Stewart of an affair in which the detachment under his command was engaged on the 13th instant whilst attached to Major Raikes' column (see October 6th) in the neighbourhood of Jellalpore on the Tonse river. Lieutenant Stewart's arrangements on this occasion appear to have been perfectly satisfactory and made with great promptitude, and though the hasty flight of the enemy prevented the detachment from inflicting any great loss upon them, yet both Lieutenant Stewart and Lieutenant Forlong have entitled themselves to Major Vaughan's approbation and thanks. Major Vaughan has further the

Affair near Jellalpore in which Lieutenant Stewart's detachment was engaged.

gratification of recording that Major Raikes has assured him that the
conduct of the detachment whilst under his command was most
admirable."

Lord Clyde's Byswara Campaign. On the 26th of October 1858, what is generally called
" Lord Clyde's Byswara Campaign " commenced, the regiment
retaining its place in Brigadier A. Horsford's Brigade of Sir
Hope Grant's Division.

Force arrives before Amethee. On the 9th of November 1858 the force arrived before
the fort of Amethee with the full expectation of forcing the
siege of that place. Rája Mádho Singh, however, surrendered
the following day.

Force arrives at Shankargarh. On the 15th November 1858 the whole force was united
before Shankargarh, the stronghold of Rája Banee Mádho
Singh, with the expectation of having to besiege that place, but
the garrison evacuated it during the right.

Two companies detached. *22nd November* 1858.—The 1st and 2nd Companies under
Lieutenant S. J. Browne and Lieutenant L. J. H. Grey (who
had joined the regiment on the 31st ultimo, were directed to
join a small detached force under Lieutenant-Colonel Galway
of the Madras Fusiliers. Colonel Galway's detachment was
engaged with the enemy on the day following, when the two
companies of the regiment rendered excellent service in pur-
suing a party of rebels from the fort of Rehora on the Goomtee to that of Kœlhee about 2 miles higher up the river. In
this affair the regiment had two casualties, one fatal (see G.
O. C. C., p. 1797, of 1858, dated 31st October 1858),—Sepoy
Hira Singh killed, 1 Havildár wounded.

Regimental head-quarters march to reinforce Colonel Galway. Lieutenant-Colonel Galway having applied for reinforcements to enable him to expel the enemy from the fort of
Kœlhee, the head-quarters of the regiment, with a heavy
battery and other troops, marched on the night of the 23rd
November 1858 against that fort, but the rebels had evacuated
it during the night.

Regiment joins Commander-in-Chief's camp. On the 19th December 1858 the regiment joined the
Commander-in-Chief's camp at Bahraich.

Regimental Order, dated Camp Bahraich, 21st December 1858.

Regiment detached under Colonel Christie.

4 Guns, Bengal Horse Artillery.	" With reference to G. O. C. C. of this day, the regiment will march immediately with the force noted in the margin under the command of Colonel Christie, Her Majesty's 80th Regiment."
Detachment Hodson's Horse.	
5 Companies, Her Majesty's 80th Regiment.	
2 Companies. Her Majesty's 20th Regiment.	

The object, it is understood, of detaching this column was to clear the country between the Chota Sarjoo and Gogra rivers, in furtherance of the general plan of the campaign for driving the rebels into the Nepal territory by the course of the Raptee. Having marched northwards as far as Pudnaha, the column rejoined the Commander-in-Chief's camp at Bankee on the 4th of January 1859.

Regiment rejoins Commander-in-Chief's Camp.

Regimental Order, dated Camp Sidonia Ghât, 7th January 1859.

"With reference to Brigade Orders of this date, the regiment will furnish a party of 1 Jemadár, 2 Havildárs, 2 Naicks and 24 Privates for the purpose of escorting a prisoner, the Nawáb of Furruckabad, towards Cawnpore."

Party furnished to escort a State prisoner.

The great object of the campaign having been achieved by the expulsion of the main body of rebels from Oudh into the Nepal territory, the army was broken up and re-distributed, a considerable force of all arms, including the regiment, remaining under Brigadier Horsford's command at Sidonia Ghât on the Raptee to prevent the return of the rebels into Oudh.

The army broken up and a force left at Sidonia Ghât to which the regiment is attached.

Regimental Order No. 619, dated Camp Sidonia Ghât, 12th January 1859.

"With reference to Brigade Orders of this date, directing the troops 80 Sabres, 1st Punjab Cavalry. 3 Companies, 2nd Battalion, Rifle Brigade. 5th Punjab Infantry. noted in the margin to march on a special service under the command of Major J. L. Vaughan at 11-15 P.M., the regiment will strike camp at 10 P.M."

The regiment proceeds on special service.

The above service was accomplished by driving a party of rebels out of a position they had taken up at the Koronia Sota, a deep nullah or ravine, the bed of which forms an indifferent road through the low range of hills which forms the boundary between Oudh and the Sonar Valley (Nepal).

Affair at Koronia Sota.

8th February 1859.—Orders having been received from Government for the advance into Nepal territory of Brigadier Horsford's force from Sidonia Ghât, in view to drive the rebels from a very strong position they had taken up at Sitka Ghât on the Raptee, the following Regimental Order was issued:—

Brigadier Horsford's force advances into Nepal.

"With reference to Brigade army Orders, the regiment will march to-morrow morning towards the Nepal frontier, and will head the column."

Regimental Order No. 679, dated Camp Sissowah, Nepal territory, 9th February 1859.

"The Commanding Officer congratulates the regiment on the share taken by it in the capture of the rebels' position at Sitka Ghât

Rebels' position at Sitka captured with 14 guns.

yesterday, when 16 guns fell into our hands. The steadiness, obedience, and yet eagerness of all ranks to engage the enemy were most conspicuous."

(See Brigadier Horsford's despatch published in G. G. O. No. 347, dated 14th March 1859.)

A wing of the regiment sent forward to reconnoitre up to the Deokurh Valley.   On the 11th February 1859 the head-quarters and left wing of the regiment were detached from Brigadier Horsford's force to reconnoitre the road as far as the Deokurh Valley, which lies to the eastward of the Sonar Valley. The line of march in executing this duty lay contiguous to the course of the Raptee, which river was crossed at Sita Ghât, the scene of the engagement on the 8th. The road was found strewed with broken hackeries (country carts) and other signs of the hasty retreat of the rebel force. The wing encamped on the night of the 12th February in very heavy rain at Koosamba, about 16 miles from Brigadier Horsford's camp, and the next morning Major Vaughan rode forward until the Deokurh Valley could be seen, accompanied by a small picked body of men from the wing. The required information as to the nature of the road and the condition of the rebels having been thus obtained, the regiment marched on the 14th to rejoin the camp. On the 17th the whole of the force returned to Sidonia Ghât and encamped in British territory.

Regiment arrives at Bahraich.   *7th March* 1859.—The force under Brigadier Horsford having been broken up, the regiment reached the quarters assigned to it, Bahraich, this day, having left two companies at Nanpara under Lieutenant Grey.

Regimental Order No. 44, dated Camp Bahraich, 3rd April 1859.

Regiment marches with a force.   With reference to Field Force Order of this date, the regiment will march this afternoon at 3 o'clock with the force noted in the margin, the whole under the command of Major J. L. Vaughan. No. 1 Company, under the command of Lieutenant S. J. Browne, will remain at Bahraich.

> 2 Guns, B. H. A.
> 1st Punjab Cavalry.
> 2 Companies, 1st Battalion, Rifle Brigade.
> 5th Punjab Infantry.

Object of the move.   The object of the above move was to prevent the rebels, who had met with a severe repulse from a force operating in the Gorakhpur district, from re-entering British territory by any of the Trans-Raptee passes, as they appeared disposed to do. The column of which the regiment formed part was charged with the defence of the line of the Upper Raptee, namely, from where the Raptee enters British territory near Sidonia Ghât to Bhingah 30 miles lower down.

After repelling an attempt made by a considerable body of rebels to cross the Raptee at Sidonia Ghât on the 3rd of April 1859, the force went into standing camp at Sidonia Ghât, throwing out pickets at the village of Pehrari, five or six miles from camp, to watch the main road from Nepal. A little work was constructed at this village (which is situated in a small clearing in the dense Terai forest) by the men's labour, and was found most effectually to control the roads, and ensure information of the rebel movements in that direction.

Repulse of the rebels at Sidonia Ghat.

On the 12th of April 1859 the 1st Company, which had been left at Bahraich on the march of the head-quarters with Major J. L. Vaughan's field force, took part in an encounter with some rebels in the neighbourhood of Akonah. In this affair Lieutenant S. J. Browne's charger was wounded and one private killed (see G. G. O. No. 804, dated 3rd June 1859)—Sepoy Hira Singh, No. 1 Company.

No. 1 Company takes part in an affair near Akonah.

On the 25th of April 1859 the 4th and 7th Companies, which had joined a force under the personal command of Brigadier Horsford, c.b., took part in an affair with a large body of rebels in the jungles between the Gurwa and the Kooreallee rivers, and obtained great commendation from the Brigadier for their conduct. In this affair Lieutenant Forlong, who commanded the companies, behaved with great spirit in a personal encounter, and both his name and that of Captain W. D. Hoste (who had been acting as Brigade Quartermaster to Brigadier Horsford's Brigade since November 1858) were favourably mentioned in despatches (see G. G. O. No. 823, dated 7th June 1859).

Nos. 4 and 7 Companies take part in an affair under the personal command of Brigadier Horsford.

Subadár Aziz Khan, 4th Company, obtained the 3rd Class of the Order of Merit for his gallantry on this and sundry other occasions.

Order of Merit, 3rd Class, conferred on Subadar Aziz Khan.

30th April 1859.—This day for the third time the head-quarters of the regiment entered the Nepal territory in pursuit of a large body of rebels, the fugitives from Brigadier Horsford's affair of the 25th. The infantry were halted after proceeding about 12 miles, but the cavalry and horse artillery followed the rebels as far as Sitka Ghât and exchanged shots with them across the river.

Pursuit of a body of rebels to Sitka Ghat.

Regimental Order No. 95, dated Sidonia Ghát, 14th May 1859.

Nos. 8 and 9 Companies take part in the defeat of the rebels at Koronia Sota. "The Commanding Officer has great pleasure in placing upon record his satisfaction at the spirit displayed by the 8th and 9th Companies in action with a party of rebels at Koronia Sota yesterday under the command of Lieutenant and Adjutant C. E. Stewart.

"It deserves to be recorded that, besides engaging the enemy and inflicting great loss upon them, these companies marched 48 miles between 3 A.M. and 9 P.M. at the hottest season of the year."

The rebel leader Bakht Khan slain. In the above affair the notorious rebel leader Bakht Khan, once a Subadár in the Bengal Artillery, and afterwards a prime mover in the mutiny of the Bareilly Brigade, and for a time Generalissimo in Delhi during the siege, was slain by Naick Habíbullah Khan and Private Fukír Shah of the 9th Company. Both these men obtained the 3rd Class of the Order of Merit for their conduct on the occasion.

(For the official report of the above affair see G. O. G. G. No. 840, dated 14th June 1859.) Sepoy Azád Khan, No. 10 Company, killed.

Regimental Order No. 132, dated Camp Banhouse, 14th June 1859.

Affair in the Kangra Pass leading into Nepal. "The Commanding Officer heartily congratulates the regiment on the excellent service that it has done to-day in driving a large number of rebels under Purgan Singh out of British territory. The conduct of all was excellent. The regiment had marched 32 miles the night before and 20 miles last night before engaging the enemy; yet the pursuit was urged with a spirit which left nothing to be desired, and only ceased when the rebels were utterly broken and dispersed. The Commanding Officer will recommend Subadár Habíb Khan for the Order of Merit for his gallantry to-day. He also noticed the forward conduct of many others, which will be duly noted in the regimental records for future reference."

(For the official report of the above affair see G. O. G. G. No. 1073, dated 25th July 1859.)

Regimental Order No. 137, dated Camp Musha, 17th June 1859.

Regiment marches on special service. "The regiment will get under arms immediately in view to proceeding on a special service. Camp will be left standing."

Regimental Order No. 138, dated Camp Musha, 18th June 1859.

Affair in the Sumpatri Pass leading into Nepal. "The Commanding Officer again congratulates the regiment on the excellent service it has this day rendered in expelling from British territory with great loss a body of rebels who had located themselves in the Sumpatri Pass leading into Nepal. The spirit evinced by all ranks in this fatiguing service was beyond praise, and was crowned, as it deserved to be, by signal success, as the number of rebels slain and of horses and baggage animals captured sufficiently testifies."

(For the official account of the above affair see G. O. G. G. No. 153, dated 22nd July 1859.)

For their conduct in the two above affairs the following Native Officers, &c., of the regiment were admitted to the 3rd Class of the Order of Merit :— *Native Officers, &c., admitted to the 3rd Class of the Order of Merit.*

Subadár Habíb Khan. | Havildár Músah Khan.
Subadár Nihál Singh. |

On the 24th June 1859 the camp at Sidonia Ghát was broken up under orders from Major-General Sir J. Hope Grant, Commanding the Oudh Division, and the regiment returned to Bahraich, where lines had been built for it under the superintendence of Lieutenant S. J. Browne, Doing Duty Officer. *Regiment proceeds to Bahraich.*

Regimental Order No. 255, dated 15th September 1859.

"Captain W. D. Hoste having been permitted to resign his appointment of Officiating 2nd-in-Command, he is struck off the rolls of the regiment. It is with sincere regret that Lieutenant-Colonel Vaughan makes the above announcement to the regiment, and he is certain that all ranks under him will be equally sorry. *Captain W. D. Hoste leaves the regiment.*

"It is not in the language of mere cold official conventionalism, but with heartfelt sincerity that Lieutenant-Colonel Vaughan records his sense of the loss the regiment sustains by Captain Hoste's leaving it, and his hope that, wherever his future lot is cast, success and happiness may attend him.

In furtherance of arrangements made by Brigadier Holdich, C.B., Commanding the Troops Trans-Gogra, for the final capture and dispersion of the rebels who had taken refuge in the Nepal territories, detachments of the regiment were posted during the months of November and December 1859 at various points on the Raptee to prevent the rebels, when pressed in rear by the Nepal troops, from crossing that river into Oudh. Three companies marched from Bahraich on this service to Akonah on the 4th of November, two companies to Pípri Ghát near Bingah on the 12th of November, and three companies to Nanparah on the 25th of November. The defence of the entire line of the Upper Raptee from Akonah upwards was confided to Lieutenant-Colonel Vaughan. *Final proceedings against the rebels.*

Regimental Order No. 352. dated Bahraich, 29th December 1859.

Field Force Orders on the conclusion of the operations.

"The following extract from Field Force Orders by Brigadier Holdich, C.B., Commanding Trans-Gogra and Gorakhpur Districts, is recorded for information :—

Camp Khukoria, dated 26th December 1859.

"*No.* 6.—A detachment of 250 men of the Moradabad Levy will proceed from Nanpara to Bahraich to relieve the 5th Punjab Infantry.

"*No.* 7.—Under instructions from Divisional Head-Quarters the 5th Punjab Rifles, on being relieved by a detachment of the Moradabad Levy, will march to Cawnpore *en route* to Lahore.

"Lieutenant-Colonel Vaughan will report direct to the Quarter-master-General of the Army the probable date of his moving, and also (by telegraph) his arrival at Cawnpore, where he will halt until distinct orders are received by him from Army Head-Quarters.

"On the departure of the 5th Punjab Rifles from the Oudh frontier district, the Brigadier would record his appreciation of the services rendered by Lieutenant-Colonel Vaughan and the regiment under his command.

"To Lieutenant-Colonel Vaughan was confided the distribution of the troops in the Bahraich district during the late combined operations with the Nepalese against the rebels in the Terai. His arrangements were such as effectually to prevent any escape of the rebels across the Raptee.

"The services of the 5th Punjab Rifles in former campaigns are well known, and for those rendered in recent operations Brigadier Holdich begs to offer his best thanks to Lieutenant-Colonel Vaughan and the officers and men under his command."

Government letter thanking the troops engaged in the final dispersion of the rebels.

In view to complete the record of the services of the regiment in Hindustán, the following record and memorandum may be appropriately entered in this place :—

From Major-General R. J. H. BIRCH, Secretary to the Government of India, Military Department, to the Adjutant-General of the Army, No. 94, dated 1st February 1860.

"Having laid before His Excellency the Governor-General your letter No. 23 A. of the 7th ultimo, transmitting a despatch from Brigadier Holdich, C.B., Commanding the Gorakhpur and Oudh Frontier, reporting the termination of active operations against the rebels on the Nepal border, I am directed to request that the Right Hon'ble the Commander-in-Chief may be moved to cause the special acknowledgments of His Excellency to be conveyed to Brigadier Holdich, C.B., for his excellent and most successful services, and to the whole of the officers and men, European and Native, who served under his command for the energy and zeal displayed by them on all occasions during the period above stated."

Memo. by Lieutenant-Colonel W. MAYHEW, Adjutant-General of the Army.

The above forwarded to Colonel Holdich, C.B., for information and communication to the troops lately under his command.

Memo. by Colonel E. A. HOLDICH, late Brigadier Commanding Trans-Gogra Brigade.

Forwarded to the Officer Commanding 5th Punjab Rifles, for communication to the officers and men of that corps who were engaged in the late operations on the Nepal border.

On the 27th of December 1859 the following Circular was received at Regimental Head-Quarters, and the terms on which the regiment was invited to volunteer for service in China were explained at parade on the following morning :— *Regiment called upon to volunteer for service in China.*

Circular by Major-General R. J. H. BIRCH, Secretary to the Government of India, Military Department, dated 20th December 1859.

" The Officer Commanding the 5th Regiment Punjab Infantry is requested to inform the Commander-in-Chief by telegram, addressed to the Assistant Adjutant-General of the Army at Head-Quarters, whether the 5th Punjab Infantry is inclined to volunteer for foreign service in China according to the terms of the General Order by the Governor-General, No. 52, dated 20th December 1859.

" It will be understood that whilst Government desire to know the wishes of the 5th Punjab Infantry as a body, the precautions necessary to ascertain the individual willingness of the sepoys to proceed on the service indicated will be taken hereafter under certain instructions as per paragraph 7 of the Government Order, when the decision of the Government shall have been made as to the particular regiments selected."

From Lieut.-Colonel J. L. VAUGHAN, Commanding 5th Regiment Punjab Infantry, to the Secretary to the Government of India, Military Department, No. 301, dated Camp Bahraich, 29th December 1859.

" I have the honor to acknowledge the receipt of your Circular under date 20th December, enclosing copy of G. O. G. G. No. 52 of same date. *Report of the result of the volunteering.*

" The terms of the G. O. have been most carefully explained to the regiment, and I have reported by telegram this day that more than two-thirds of the men are desirous to proceed to China. I have 678 of all ranks at head-quarters ; of these 475 volunteer and 203 do not. The sentiments of 137 of all ranks on furlough have of course not been ascertained."

Regimental Order, dated Camp Cawnpore, 14th January 1860.

Regiment paraded before Sir J. Inglis, K.C.B.

" Under instructions from Major-General Sir John Inglis, K.C.B., Commanding the Division, the regiment will parade at 2 P.M. for the purpose of men who volunteer for China giving in and signing their names."

Result.

The result of the volunteering was that 385 signed to go to China and 292 refused ; about 90 men who had volunteered on the 28th of December withdrew when the option was again given on the 14th of January 1860.

Behaviour of the different classes.

The Sikhs showed a much greater readiness to go to China than the other classes, *viz.*, Patháns, Punjabi Muhammadans and Dográs.

Remarks on the volunteering.

The result of the volunteering (though matter of the greatest disappointment to the British Officers of the regiment) was, under the circumstances, not surprising. The regiment had been in the field for more than two years and a half, and had had no regular cantonment for almost three. At the very time the volunteering took place the men received six months' batta, in consideration of the corps having been constantly in the field for more than two years, and having rendered valuable service (*vide* Government letter No. 899, dated Council Chamber, Fort William, 22nd September 1859); they had also acquired much money by plunder. Finally, the men felt with justice that they had honourably completed the service for which they had been sent out of the Punjab, and were not unnaturally disinclined to *volunteer* for a new and remote service.

Regimental Order, dated Camp Cawnpore, 26th January 1860.

The regiment ordered to proceed towards Lahore.

" Under instructions received from Divisional Head-Quarters, the regiment will march to-morrow towards Kalliánpur, *en route* to Lahore."

The regiment arrives at Kohat.

At Lahore orders were received that the regiment was to go to Kohát and be cantoned there. It arrived at the latter place on the 11th of April 1860 and was quartered in the Right Infantry Barracks.

Regiment ordered to Dera Ismail Khan.

On the 22nd March 1861 the regiment received the order to march to Dera Ismail Khan, there to be stationed as soon as Lieutenant-Colonel Vaughan should rejoin from furlough.

On the 25th of March 1861 and the following days the *Regiment inspected by Lieutenant-Colonel Wilde, C.B.* regiment was inspected by Lieutenant-Colonel Wilde, C.B., Commanding at Kohát, by order of Brigadier-General Chamberlain, C.B., Commanding the Force.

On the 10th of April 1861 the regiment commenced its *The regiment marches towards Dera Ismail Khan.* march towards Dera Ismail Khan.

20th April 1861.—On arrival at Peyzu this day 368 of all *Three hundred and sixty-eight men proceeded to frontier posts.* ranks were detailed to proceed to Tánk under command of Lieutenant C. E. Stewart, and take over the duties of the frontier posts, in relief of the 6th Regiment Punjab Infantry.

23rd April 1861.—On this date the head-quarters of *Arrival at Dera Ismail Khan.* the regiment arrived at Dera Ismail Khan. From this time until the termination of the blockade of the Mahsúd Wazíris in the autumn of the year, the regiment, in conjunction with the 6th Punjab Infantry, furnished the very strong infantry detail (as above) required for the defence of the frontier posts. During this period a party from the Gomal Outpost took part in an affair with Wazíri plunderers in the Zirummi Pass, when three or four of the latter were killed and several others made prisoners. On the cessation of the blockade the frontier duties were considerably lightened, though they still employed a large number of men.

12th February 1862.—The regiment paraded in brigade *Parade before Sir Hugh Rose, Commander-in-Chief.* with the other troops at the station for the inspection of His Excellency Sir Hugh Rose, G.C.B., Commander-in-Chief in India.

10th April 1862.—The regiment paraded in heavy march- *Inspected by Brigadier-General Neville Chamberlain.* ing order for the inspection of Brigadier-General Neville Chamberlain, C.B., Commanding the Force, who was pleased to express his approval of its general appearance and steadiness under arms.

The only other matters which call for remarks during *Reduction of the establishment and revised composition of the regiment.* the service of the regiment on the Dera Ismail Khan frontier are, 1st, that, in accordance with G. G. O. No. 400 of 1861, the establishment was reduced from 10 to 8 companies, in consequence of which the 6th and 7th Companies were broken up. The same order abolished the office of Native Adjutant, and instituted instead the grade of Subadár-Major. Native Adjutant Subadár Lál Khan resigned the service upon the abolition of his appointment, and Subadár Jewan Singh (the senior Subadár) was appointed Subadár-Major.

2nd.—The composition of the regiment was altered in consequence of the reduction of two companies, and the following was laid down by the Brigadier-General Commanding as the future composition of the regiment :—

> 3 Companies Sikhs.
> 3   „   Pathána.
> 1 Company Punjabi Muhammadans.
> 1   „   Dogras.

3rd.—The whole of the combatant officers of the regiment enrolled themselves in the Bengal Staff Corps formed on the amalgamation of Her Majesty's British and Indian Forces.

Regiment marches towards Kohat.   *25th November* 1862.—The regiment commenced its march towards Kohát, the station assigned to it, at the general relief of 1862-63.

Arrival at Kohat.   *9th December* 1862.—The regiment marched into the Kohát Cantonment.

Regimental Order, dated 3rd January 1863.

Distribution of the Indian Mutiny Medal.   "The regiment will parade at 12 o'clock (noon) to-morrow for the distribution of the Indian Mutiny Medal to those entitled to receive it."

Inspection.   *29th April* 1863.—The regiment was inspected by Brigadier-General Sir Neville Chamberlain, K.C.B., Commanding the Force.

The regiment marches to join the Eusafzai Field Force.   *7th October* 1863.—The regiment marched to join the Yusafzai Field Force, formed for service against the Hindustáni fanatics of Mulka who had lately re-occupied Sittana, no attempt to prevent this being made by the Utmanzai and Gadún tribes, who had in 1858 entered into an engagement with the British Government that they would not allow the re-settlement in their territories of the Hindustánis, who now commenced sending robbers into Hazára to carry off Hindu baniahs, threatening raids, and Maulvi Abdulla, with the other Syad leaders, preaching a "jehad" or religious war. It was therefore considered absolutely necessary to have recourse to military operations and that at once, as delay, which with these tribes is little understood, might encourage others to action, and a favorable opportunity might thus be lost for putting an end to the chronic frontier irritation which existed. An expedition was accordingly sanctioned, the first object being to effectually rid the frontier of the Hindustáni fanatics.

Their mere expulsion from the right bank of the Indus back
upon their old posts at Mulka, and on the south bank of the
Barando, was not considered enough, nor was it advisable that
they should find shelter in Swát, and make that powerful tribe the future focus of disturbance. If possible, the
line of retreat of the fanatics towards Barando was to be
cut off, and although their extirpation might not be possible,
yet their dispersion would be on lines of direction favourable
to their capture, if the co-operation of the well-disposed sections
of the tribe could be elicited. The punishment of the
Gadúns was to be quite a secondary consideration to the primary
one of crushing that small but troublesome horde of fanatics.

The plan of operations decided on by Sir Neville
Chamberlain, K.C.B., Commanding, was to push through the
Umbeyla Pass into Bonair, and thus force the Hindustánis
to fight with their backs to the plains,—operating in fact on
their line of retreat. But taking up a position in the Chamba
Valley, a force would be able to take its stand in open ground,
in rear of the whole of the enemy's tract, which it would fully
command, and from whence, by rapid excursions, it would be
able to do all its work and deal with all difficulties, returning
when convenient to its standing camp, while such a position
would render the tribes on the southern slopes of the Mahában
well nigh powerless. No hostilities were anticipated from the
Bonairwals to the temporary encamping of the force in the
Chamba Valley, as it was known that they had no sympathies
with the fanatics, being of different tenets, and forming part
of the religious constituency of the Akhoond of Swát, who at
that time was bitterly opposed to the Hindustánís, calling
them Wahábís. These anticipations of no opposition from the
tribes were, however, not verified, as the sequel will show.

On the 20th of October 1863 the regiment formed part
of the advance column under Lieutenant-Colonel Wilde, C.B.,
which obtained possession of the crest of the Umbeyla Pass
with slight opposition. On the night of the 22nd it reinforced
the upper left pickets of the camp, and assisted in repelling the
attack of the enemy. From the last named date it was permanently attached to the left defences of the camp, and took a
prominent part in the severe action fought at the upper left
defences on the 26th October. No. 4 Company, under Lieutenant Beckett's command, behaved with remarkable steadiness

on this occasion when employed to support and cover the
retirement of the 6th Punjab Infantry.

" On this occasion Sir Neville Chamberlain reported that Lieutenant-Colonel Vaughan's management of the troops was excellent, and
he considered himself indebted to his clear judgment for the very successful result of the action * * * that the 5th Punjab Infantry, under
Lieutenant Stewart, had been chiefly employed to cover and support the
guns, one company of which, under Lieutenant Beckett, did excellent
service in supporting the advance of the 6th Punjab Infantry, and that
it had withdrawn in the best order after the 6th Punjab Infantry
regained its position."

**Holds the
" Eagle's
Nest " Pick-
et.** On the 29th of October the regiment was told off to occupy permanently the picket known as the " Eagle's Nest," and
continued to hold this exposed and most important post under
a constant fire from the enemy's marksmen on the Guru
**The with-
drawal from
the Guru
Mountain.** Mountain until the morning of the 18th November, when the
whole of the pickets on the Guru were withdrawn and the
force concentrated on the opposite or south side of the Pass.
Lieutenant Beckett, with Subadár Aziz Khan and a portion
of No. 4 Company, which had behaved with such steadiness
on the 26th of October, held the " Eagle's Nest " during the
withdrawal, and did not retire till the rest of the regiment
had reached the station of the next of the chain of pickets
forming the left defences of the position.

**Share in the
occurrences
of the 18th
Novem-
ber.** Tired as the men and officers were from holding the key
of the left defences (the Eagle's Nest Picket) for three weeks,
they were employed throughout the 18th of November in assist-
ing to construct a new work called the " Water Picket," and
the left front of the new position having been hotly threatened
by the enemy late in the evening, they were placed during the
night to defend a most exposed point, which was totally
unprotected by breastworks. During the day of the 18th a
company of the regiment under Lieutenant Fox was sent as a
reinforcement to a picket which was hardly pressed, and did
good service.

**Share in the
re-taking of
the Crag
Picket on
the 20th.** On the 20th of November, so much of the regiment (about
220 men) as could be spared from the defences of the upper
camp took part in the recovery of the Crag Picket when it was
for the third time captured by the enemy. Brigadier-General
Sir Neville Chamberlain recorded in his despatch, dated the 21st
of November, that " Lieutenant Beckett was one of the first
to reach the summit, and also foremost in entering the work
on the left."

Lieutenant-Colonel Vaughan, who commanded one of the columns of attack, was wounded on this occasion.

From this period (the 20th of November) until the close of the operations (23rd December) the regiment formed a portion of the troops composing the advanced position, or the "upper camp."

On the 1st December, the force having been divided into two Brigades, and Lieutenant-Colonel Vaughan appointed to the temporary command of the 1st Brigade, the command of the regiment was placed in the hands of Lieutenant F. J. Keen, but this arrangement only continued until the 5th of December, when Lieutenant-Colonel Vaughan resumed the command.

About this time the following Native Officers and Non-Commissioned Officers were admitted to the Order of Merit for distinguished conduct :—

Subadár Aziz Khan to the 2nd Class for the gallantry displayed by him on the recapture of the Crag Picket on the 20th November.

Jemadár Rehmán Khan for the gallantry he showed in endeavouring to save a British soldier of the 101st Bengal Fusiliers during the retreat out of the Crag Picket on the 20th November, on which occasion he was badly wounded.

Havildár Sher Gool to the 3rd Class for the gallantry he displayed in trying to save the life of a British soldier on the same occasion.

On the 15th of December a portion of the force advanced against the enemy in the direction of Lulloo and Umbeyla, and Major-General Garvock, who had succeeded Sir Neville Chamberlain, having thought fit to place Lieutenant-Colonel Vaughan in command of the whole of the troops remaining in camp, it was not judged convenient that the regiment should form part of the advancing force.

The camp, however, having been attacked in the afternoon of the 15th, an opportunity for doing gallant service was afforded to No. 8 Company under Lieutenant Fox. The company had been sent to reinforce what was known as the "advanced picket," and joined in a very gallant charge made

(margin notes)
Lieutenant-Colonel Vaughan wounded.

Regiment takes a share in the defences of the upper camp.

Lieutenant-Colonel Vaughan appointed to the command of 1st Brigade.

Two Native Officers and one Non-Commissioned Officer admitted to the Order of Merit.

Events of the 15th December 1863.

by the rest of the picket upon the enemy, when they were
much discouraged by the ill-success of their attempts upon
the camp.

Jemadar Juma Khan admitted to the 3rd Class of the Order of Merit.

Jemadár Juma Khan received the 3rd Class of the Order
of Merit for his distinguished gallantry on this occasion.

Regiment returns to Kohat.

On the 23rd December 1863, on the breaking up of the
Yusafzai Field Force, the regiment was ordered to return to
its station (Kohát) without delay.

Lieutenant C. E. Stewart virtually Commandant of the regiment in the Umbeyla Campaign.

It would be unfair to complete the above short record of
the history of the regiment during the Umbeyla Campaign
without placing on record that Lieutenant C. E. Stewart, 2nd-
in-Command, was the virtual Commandant of the regiment
throughout the whole of the operations. Lieutenant-Colonel
Vaughan was employed as Field Officer of the left pickets and
in command of the camp defences on the side of the Guru
Mountain, and from 18th November to the 5th of December
he commanded the "advanced position" or "upper camp;"
again from and after the 15th December he commanded the
troops left in position on the Umbeyla heights; upon
Lieutenant C. E. Stewart therefore devolved all the respon-
sibility of the regimental command.

Nature of service performed by the regiment.

The regiment had not the opportunity during the operations of performing those brilliant services rendered by some
regiments of the Force, but a more than ordinary share of
harassing picket and outpost duty fell to its share (witness its
occupation of the "Eagle's Nest" picket from the 29th of
October to the 18th of November), which it performed with
unfailing cheerfulness, nor was the regiment in any instance
found wanting when opportunity for more brilliant service
offered.

Loss of the regiment.

The loss of the regiment in the operations was as
follows :—

Killed, 8 rank and file—

Havildár Syadwáli.	Sepoy Habeed.
Naick Rukkun-ud-dín.	„ Juma Khan.
Sepoy Sookoo.	„ Muhammad Dín.
„ Bahabool Khan.	„ Fattah.

Wounded, 1 European, 2 Native Officers and 16 rank and file—

Colonel J. L. Vaughan.	Sepoy Ramzán.
Jemadár Elahi Bakhsh.	„ Jamál Dín.
„ Rahman Khan.	„ Fattah Khan.
Naick Kadir Bakhsh.	„ Suchetah.
Sepoy Zareeb Khan.	„ Niáz Gul.
„ Syad Muhammad.	„ Fakir.
„ Nek Muhammad.	„ Mirzakee.
„ Fakir Khan.	„ Nek Muhammad, II.
„ Pir Bakhsh.	Langree Gurmukh Singh.
„ Hyat.	

Regimental Order, dated 6th March 1864.

"Lieutenant Beckett having this day been struck off the rolls of the regiment on removal to a higher appointment, Lieutenant-Colonel Vaughan has great pleasure in acknowledging the excellent and zealous service which he has invariably rendered whilst attached to the regiment, whether in the field or in quarters. Lieutenant-Colonel Vaughan represents the feeling of all ranks in the regiment in expressing his regret that Lieutenant Beckett ceases to be a member of the 5th Punjab Infantry."

25th April 1864.—The regiment paraded with the other troops in the garrison for the inspection of Brigadier-General Wilde, C.B., Commanding the Force. After parade the Brigadier-General conferred their decorations, as members of the Order of Merit, 3rd Class, on Jemadár Rehmán Khan and Jemadár Sher Gool (see *ante*).

29th May 1864.—On this date the following regimental order was issued:—

"With reference to G. O. G. G. No. 280 of 1864, conferring increased pay on four Subadárs and four Jemadárs, the following Native Officers of the regiment are admitted to the superior rates of pay as under:—

To the highest rate, Rs. 100 per mensem—
Subadár Khazán Singh, No. 6 Company.
„ Aziz Khán, No. 4 Company.
To the next highest rate, Rs. 80 per mensem—
Subadár-Major Jeewan Singh, No. 1 Company.
„ Pir Shah, No. 2 Company.

23rd March 1865.—The annual inspection of the regiment by Brigadier-General A. T. Wilde, C.B., Commanding the Force, commenced and was continued on subsequent days.

The regiment made the best shooting this year of the whole of the infantry regiments of the Force, as was afterwards officially notified.

Death of Lieutenant Tytler.

19th July 1865.—Intelligence was received of the death of Lieutenant and Adjutant R. C. S. C. Tytler whilst on leave. The following regimental order was issued on the occasion :—

" It is with the greatest regret that Colonel Vaughan announces to the regiment the death at Srinagar in Kashmir of Lieutenant and Adjutant R. C. S. C. Tytler, and Colonel Vaughan is sure that every officer and man in the regiment will participate in the feelings with which he makes the sad announcement. During the few years he had been attached to the regiment Lieutenant Tytler had succeeded in obtaining the esteem and regard of all ranks, and had given every promise of a useful and, if opportunity offered, distinguished career in the service.

" As a mark of respect to the deceased, officers will be pleased to wear the usual mourning for one month."

Twenty mules drafted to the Bhootan Force.

12th August 1865.—Twenty mules of the regimental cattle establishment were given over to the use of the Bhootan Expeditionary Force.

Parade to receive the Lieutenant-Governor of the Punjab.

7th December 1865.—The regiment paraded with the other troops in the garrison to receive the Lieutenant-Governor of the Punjab, who was accompanied by the Brigadier-General Commanding.

Regimental Order, dated 25th January 1866,

Pattern of linen clothing altered.

" The summer clothing requiring renewal, the pattern of coat laid down in the Dress Regulations of the Force is to be adopted in the regiment."

(The pattern hitherto in use had been a blouse, plaited front.)

Camp for hill skirmishing.

16th April 1866.—The regiment went into camp for practice in hill skirmishing.

The regiment returns to Kohat.

26th April 1866.—The regiment returned to cantonments at Kohát.

Regiment marches to Bannu.

26th May 1866.—The regiment commenced its march towards Bannu in course of relief.

Arrival at Bannu.

1st June 1866.—The regiment arrived at Bannu and was quartered in the fort.

12*th February* 1867.—The annual inspection of the regiment by the Brigadier-General Commanding the Force commenced. The following extract from a letter to the Commanding Officer by order of the Brigadier-General on the 12th of March shows the result of the inspection :— Annual inspection.

" The regiment looked as well as formerly, and the men are a fine soldier-like body, steady, clean and well dressed. You have succeeded in effecting with your regiment what under the present system of drill it is so difficult to obtain, and without which perfection a Native regiment is liable to become disorganised, if suddenly and unexpectedly attacked. You have taught the Native Officers and most of the men of the 5th Punjab Infantry to understand the object of each order and manœuvre, and whilst the regiment is one of the best Light Infantry Corps in the Punjab Frontier Force, it is one of the most silent and steady under arms."

8*th January* 1868.—The regiment marched on this date to join the Camp of Exercise at Ama Kheyl. It was there inspected by Brigadier-General A. T. Wilde, C.B., Commanding the Force, and on the breaking up of the camp returned to cantonments at Bannu. The regiment joins the Camp of Exercise at Ama Kheyl.

11*th September* 1868.—Colonel Vaughan, C.B., was appointed to command a Brigade with the rank of Brigadier-General in the Hazára Field Force, which was employed in October of the same year against the tribes of the Black Mountain. For his services on this occasion he received the special thanks of the Government. Colonel Vaughan appointed to command a Brigade in the Hazara Field Force.

Colonel Vaughan took with him Non-Commissioned Officers and privates of the regiment (all picked men), who acted as his orderlies whilst the force was actively engaged.

11*th January* 1869.—The regiment commenced its march towards Dera Ismail Khan in course of relief on this date, and arrived at that station on the 16th of January, when it took up its quarters in the Right Infantry Lines. The regiment marches in course of relief to Dera Ismail Khan.

1*st February* 1869.—Colonel J. L. Vaughan, C.B., was made Brigadier-General on the Bengal establishment and appointed to the Command of the Gwalior District. Colonel Vaughan appointed to the Command of the Gwalior Brigade.

On his leaving the Force the following Brigade Standing Order No. 3 of the 3rd of February 1869 was issued by Brigadier-General A. T. Wilde, C.B., Commanding :—

" The departure from the frontier of Colonel J. L. Vaughan, C.B., Commandant of the 5th Punjab Infantry, where he has served for 20 years, affords the Brigadier-General Commanding a fitting opportunity

of placing upon record in the annals of the Punjab Frontier Force the
long, meritorious and highly distinguishing services of this officer.
Brigadier-General J. L. Vaughan, C.B., was one of the first officers
who, after the annexation of the Punjab in 1848, assisted in the organi-
zation of the Punjab Frontier Force.

"His great professional attainments, untiring zeal and devotion
to duty soon attracted the notice of the late Sir Henry Lawrence, who
conferred on him, soon after he joined, the Command of the 5th Punjab
Infantry, which corps has become under his guidance one of the best
and most reliable regiments of the Frontier Force.

"The influence he exercised over the men he commanded, arising as
it did from his intimate knowledge of their language and their country,
was singularly tested in 1857-58, when the 5th Punjab Infantry under
Brigadier-General Vaughan's leadership were the first Native troops
in India who confronted, fought with, and defeated the rebel
native soldiers of the 55th Native Infantry at Attock and in
Eusafzai. To Brigadier-General Vaughan and his men is due the
credit of having so successfully initiated that encounter, and by display-
ing this example of fidelity he contributed in a great degree towards the
memorable services of the regiments of the Force during that most
eventful war.

"Brigadier-General Vaughan has served in most of our frontier
expeditions, and his past distinguished career and present responsible
command must be a gratifying proof to the junior officers of the Punjab
Frontier Force of the readiness of the Government to recognize and
acknowledge duty, honestly and faithfully performed in the Force to
which we belong."

The following regimental order was published by Colonel
Vaughan on his leaving the regiment :—

"In laying down the command which he has exercised for more
than 17 years, Colonel Vaughan has the proud satisfaction of feeling
that he delivers over to his successor a thoroughly loyal, contented and
efficient regiment.

"Whatever credit Colonel Vaughan may have obtained in the
course of his service as a Regimental Commandant he owes all to the
good spirit of the several ranks composing the regiment.

"He hopes and believes that the regiment will always maintain
its present high character, and that the system established will afford
the best proof of its soundness by working equally well under another
Commandant."

Regiment inspected by Briga- dier-General Hughes.
24th February 1869.—The regiment was inspected by
Brigadier-General Hughes, C.B., Commanding the Force.

Two compa- nies march to Jatta.
On the 14th January 1870 Nos. 6 and 7 Companies
marched to Jatta, on the Dera Ismail Khan border, in order to

assist in protecting the workmen employed in sinking a
well near the Girni Pass, preparatory to a post being built
there.

1st February 1870.—On this date the remainder of the
regiment marched to Jatta, arrived there on the 3rd, and
from the latter date until the 17th of March was employed in
sending out every second day upwards of 200 rifles towards
the Girni Pass to protect the workmen sinking a well.

Regiment
marches to
Jatta.

The distance from the camp to the well was upwards of
seven miles over broken and very stony ground, and, as the
detachment had to go and return on the same day, this entailed
a march of 14 miles on the men, who had to be under arms and
on the alert the whole time, as the situation was much
exposed to attack, being close under the Waziri hills.

5th February 1870.—The regiment was inspected by
Brigadier-General Hughes, c.b., Commanding the Force.

Regiment
inspected by
Brigadier-
General
Hughes.

17th March 1870.—The regiment formed a portion of
the force under Lieutenant-Colonel T. G. Kennedy, which
marched to Kot Khirgi in the low hills on the Waziri border,
and were there employed in protecting the workmen engaged
in building a larger post.

Regiment
marches to
Kot Khirgi.

The regiment remained in camp at Kot Khirgi until
the 8th of May, when, the post having been built, the troops
returned to cantonments, reaching Dera Ismail Khan on the
11th of May.

For their services at Girni and Kot Khirgi the men and
officers received the thanks of Government for the efficient
and cheerful manner in which they performed their harassing
duties, Major Jenkins and Subadár Rehmán Khan being
particularly mentioned (see Brigade Order No. 256 dated
1st September 1870).

11th January 1871.—The regiment was inspected by
Brigadier-General Keyes, c.b., Commanding the Force.

Regiment
inspected
by General
Keyes.

19th February 1871.—The regiment marched on escort
duty with the camp of His Honor the Lieutenant-Governor
of the Punjab from Chaudwán to Bannu, returning to quarters
at Dera Ismail Khan on the 20th of March, having halted for
five days at Pezoo for light infantry practice and skirmishing
with ball ammunition on the hill-side.

Regiment
goes
on escort
duty with
Lieutenant-
Governor.

Enfield rifles received.

17th *April* 1871.—The regiment was this day armed with Enfield rifles, the old 2-grooved Brunswick rifle with which the regiment had been armed many years ago being returned into store.

Frontier medal for Umbeyla received.

10th *October* 1871.—The Indian medals for Umbeyla and the North-West Frontier were received and distributed to the regiment.

Girni Pass.

24th *October* 1871.—The regiment marched to Girni, arriving there on the 28th, and until the 21st of January 1872 was employed in protecting the erection of the Girni Post at the mouth of the Girni Pass. During this time the regiment made a road from Girni to Kot Khirgi, and also erected a tower at the mouth of the pass in advance of the post. While encamped here, the whole of the hills from " Girni Sir " to Jundholah were explored by the regiment.

Regiment inspected by Brigadier-General Keyes.

20th *December* 1871.—The regiment was inspected by Brigadier-General C. P. Keyes, C.B., Commanding the Force, who ordered a present of 70 sheep to be made to the regiment " in consideration of their good work at the tower being built, and also for their soldier-like willingness and cheerful performance of all required of them."

For their services at Girni the men of the regiment shared, with the other troops employed, the thanks of both the Supreme and Punjab Governments, conveyed in letters No. 801, dated Fort William, 14th May 1872, and No. 1125, dated Lahore, 22nd April 1872.

Tank Zam Post.

22nd *January* 1872.—The regiment marched to the mouth of the Tánk Zám to protect the building of the Zam Post.

Relief by 6th Punjab Infantry and march to Dera Ghazi Khan.

20th *February* 1872.—The regiment was relieved by the 6th Punjab Infantry, and commenced its march in course of relief to Dera Gházi Khan on the 21st, at which station it arrived on the 7th of March, and took up its quarters in the Left Infantry Barracks.

Two companies detached on escort duty with Lieutenant-Governor of the Punjab.

10th *October* 1872.—Two companies, completed to full strength, left for Lahore, under the command of Captain C. E. Stewart, to form part of the escort of His Honor the Lieutenant-Governor of the Punjab during his winter tour of inspection along the frontier. The companies rejoined headquarters on the 3rd May 1873, having been constantly on the march and in camp for seven months.

7th April 1873.—The regiment was inspected by Brigadier-General C. P. Keyes, c.b , Commanding the Force.

Regiment inspec ed by Brigad er-General Keyes

18th December 1873.—The regiment was inspected by Brigadier-General C. P. Keyes, c.b., Commanding the Force.

23rd February 1874.—The regiment proceeded to the hills near Harrand on the Dera Ghází Khan frontier for light infantry practice on the hill-side. On the 28th of February it took up a position on the Kába nullah, where for a fortnight the men were daily exercised in skirmishing over the hills and firing with ball at targets placed in position on different ridges and hill-sides. On the 16th of March the regiment returned to cantonments.

Regiment marches to Harrand for light infantry practice on the hill-side.

23rd October 1874.—The regiment commenced on this date its march towards Abbott-abad, to which station it had been ordered in course of relief. It reached its destination on the 24th of November 1874.

Regiment marches to Abbott-abad.

During the winter months of 1874-75 the regiment suffered very severely from pneumonia, so much so that the musketry course had to be suspended and only the very lightest drills and duties performed.

Great sickness in the regiment.

The number of deaths from pneumonia were—

- 1   Native Officer, Jemadár Sipáhi Khan ;
- 3   Non-Commissioned Officers ;
- 15   Privates ;
- 5   Buglers ;
- 9   Camp-followers.

7th December 1874.—Three hundred and forty long Snider rifles were received and four companies were armed with them.

Regiment armed with Sniders.

19th January 1875.—On this date 340 more long Snider rifles were received, which completed the armament of all ranks with that weapon, with the exception of the Sergeants, to whom short Snider rifles were issued at a later date.

23rd June 1875.—In consequence of the tribes of the Black Mountain collecting and threatening a raid on the

Oghi Post reinforced.

Agror Valley, the regiment was called upon at a moment's
notice to send without delay a reinforce-
ment, strength as per margin, to the Oghi
Post, 40 miles off. Within less than three
hours of the receipt of the order the detachment marched from the cantonments,
taking with it camp equipage, baggage, ammunition and ten
days' supply of provisions, and, notwithstanding the very great
heat of the weather, marched the distance, 40 miles, in $13\frac{1}{4}$
hours. Only two men asked to fall out of the ranks, and they
only when within three miles of the post.

1 British Officer.
3 Native Officers.
12 Non-commissioned
   Officers.
1 Bugler.
90 Privates.

With reference to the foregoing, it is as well to add
the following extract from the Assistant Adjutant-General's
memo. No. 1852 of the 3rd of July 1875 :—

"By desire of the Brigadier-General Commanding, remarks that
the alacrity displayed by the detachment 5th Punjab Infantry in
marching to Oghi at three hours' notice in less than 14 hours on the
night of the 23rd June is very creditable both to officers and men."

Target prac-tice, 1875. In the target practice return for 1875 the regiment
stood third in the list of the whole army with a figure of merit
of 104·08, and was one of the regiments particularly complimented in General Orders by His Excellency the Commander-
in-Chief for efficiency in musketry.

Regi-ment march-es to Delhi Camp of Exercise. On the 18th of October 1875 the regiment, having
been ordered to join the Camp of Exercise at Delhi, marched
from Abbott-abad. On the 9th of December it reached Delhi,
having marched 553 miles, and was posted to the 2nd Brigade,
4th Division.

While at the Camp it was inspected both by Brigadier-
General G. C. Ross, Commanding the Brigade, and by General
Donald Stewart, Commanding the Division. It also paraded
on the 16th December for the inspection of His Excellency
Lord Napier, the Commander-in-Chief, and again on the 12th
January 1876, when the whole army was reviewed by His
Royal Highness the Prince of Wales.

Regi-ment returns to Abbott-abad. On the 18th of January 1876 the regiment commenced its return march to Abbott-abad, reaching canton-
ments on the 10th March.

Conduct of the men. During the five months the regiment was on the line
of march and at the Camp of Exercise the conduct of the men

of the corps was most exemplary, and, though subjected to sudden, and to them strange, restrictions at the Camp at Delhi, there was not a single instance of misbehaviour or infraction of Camp police rules.

Copy of remarks by Brigadier-General C. P. Keyes, c.b., Commanding Punjab Frontier Force, on the inspection of the 5th Regiment Punjab Infantry :— Inspection Report, 1876.

No. 1333, dated 24th July 1876.

" The regiment marched from Abbott-abad on the 18th October 1875, *en route* to Delhi, to join the Camp of Exercise.

" It returned to Abbott-abad on the 10th of March 1876.

" I had the pleasure of seeing the regiment work at the Camp, and as I have not the opportunity of inspecting it this year, it gives me much gratification to be able to place on record the opinions expressed by the General Officers under whose immediate command it was employed at the Camp.

" The state of discipline and general efficiency of the corps, which elicited such high praise from such distinguished officers as Major-General Stewart and Brigadier-General Ross, is highly creditable to Major McQueen and the regiment generally."

Opinion of Major-General STEWART, c.b., Commanding 4th Division, Camp of Exercise.

" It is due to Major McQueen, Commanding the 5th Punjab Infantry, that I should place on record the opinion I formed of his regiment during the time it served under my command at the Camp of Exercise lately assembled at Delhi.

" In all executive points I found the regiment to be in excellent order, and I do not hesitate to say that it is fit for any service. The men composing the corps are a remarkably fine body, and I was particularly struck with their zealous and soldier-like bearing, and the cheerfulness with which they did their work under circumstances which often exposed them to a good deal of discomfort and much real fatigue. The condition of the regiment is most creditable to Major McQueen and his officers, and I should esteem it a favor if you will cause the substance of this letter to be communicated to the regiment."

Opinion of Brigadier-General Ross, late Commanding 2nd Infantry Brigade, 4th Division, Camp of Exercise.

" During the period at the Camp of Exercise, Delhi, 1875-76, that the 5th Punjab Infantry formed portion of the Brigade under my command I formed the highest opinion of Major McQueen as Commanding Officer and of the regiment generally.

"I consider the Officers, European and Native, smart and well instructed, and the men a fine and efficient body of soldiers."

The Supreme Government also remarked in letter No. 649, dated Fort William, the 15th of November 1876, from the Secretary to the Government of India, Military Department :—

"*Para.* 14.
2nd Punjab Cavalry.
1st Punjab Infantry.
5th Punjab Infantry.

In conclusion, I am to take this opportunity of acknowledging the credit gained for the Force by the regiments which served at the late Camp at Delhi, when the fine appearance of the infantry regiments was so remarked on."

Target practice, 1876.
In the target practice return for 1876 the regiment again stood third on the list of the whole army with a figure of merit of 111·52.

Regiment moved into the Oghi Valley for field firing.
1st April 1877.—On this date the regiment marched out to the Oghi Valley for the purpose of practising skirmishing and firing with ball ammunition at targets on the hillside, but in consequence of many days of inclement rainy weather the programme could not be carried out and the regiment returned to Abbott-abad on the 16th April 1877.

Inspection.
17th April 1877.—The regiment was inspected by Brigadier-General C. P. Keyes, C.B.

Target practice, 1877.
In the target practice return for 1877 the regiment again stood third on the list of the army with a figure of merit of 117·45, and the Magdala Gold Medal was won by Sepoy Narain Singh, F. Company, 5th Punjab Infantry.

March for Shádipur for Jowaki blockade.
On the 10th October 1877 a wing of the regiment with head-quarters marched with a wing of the 5th Goorkhas to Shádipur on the Indus to take part in protecting that portion of the Kohát border from raids of the Jowáki Afrídís.

On the 20th the Shádipur column encamped at Lukka Taláo, about three miles from the border, and the Afrídís made a slight attack on one of the pickets of the regiment under Jemadár Shám Singh. They, however, very quickly retreated on the Khuttuck-Afrídi Company moving out against them. On the following morning the Shádipur column under Major McQueen moved out to reconnoitre the Numdári Pass (a very rugged, narrow defile with very commanding heights on the north side). The crest of the pass was seized without opposition, and an Afrídi picket of upwards of 20 men, who were not on the look-out, were nearly captured. After a rough sketch had been made of the Paia Valley, which was seen from the crest, the column retired covered by two companies of the regiment, the Afrídís following, but not with any great dash. Casualties *nil*.

On the 25th the column moved out and reconnoitred part of the Gaoz-durrah Valley ; only a few of the enemy were seen. On the 5th November 1877 the Nanung Pass was reconnoitred. No opposition was made by the enemy, but a few shots were fired from a long distance.

When the regiment was at Lukka Taláo the men not only made very large strong breastworks for the pickets, but also roads, and cut down an immense quantity of dense jungle round camp, which would have afforded advantageous cover to an enemy. The men were also employed in putting the villages of Shádipur, Pushtu Chunda, and Saim in a state of defence, and at the latter village the men of F. Company built a high stone tower in a couple of days. Nothing could exceed the spirit, cheerfulness and energy with which the men worked at all these fatigue duties. *The fatigue duties performed.*

On the morning of the 9th November 1877 the Shádipur Column, under the command of Colonel Gardiner, advanced through the Nanung Pass in order to co-operate with the force under General Keyes advancing from Kohát against the Jowáki Afrídís. Lieutenant J. E. Mein with a company formed the advanced guard until the enemy were met with on the heights at the crest of the pass, and as they began a brisk, smart fire a second company, under Lieutenant G. Gaisford, was sent forward, and the united companies drove the enemy from ridge to ridge in a very dashing manner. The country through which the column (covered by the 5th Punjab Infantry) now had to advance was a very dense thorn jungle intersected by large ravines, with here and there low ridges. It was a valley about 1½ miles in width with high hills on either side. The regiment skirmishing with the enemy met with no serious opposition until it had advanced about three miles from the Nanung Pass, where the enemy had taken up a strong position on a ridge with a deep ravine in front; but the men of the regiment rapidly closing with the enemy charged the hill and, driving them off, inflicted severe punishment. It was subsequently learnt that upwards of ten of the Afrídís had been killed and many wounded. After this no further *The advance into the Afrídi country.*

opposition was made to the advance of the column on Paia,
where it joined General Keyes's force, and encamped in the
hamlets of Khustu.

Major
Stewart's
Affair

On the 12th November 1877 a company under Major
C. E. Stewart, which had been sent up the Tumbal Pitao
range in order to drive off some of the enemy who were
annoying the foraging parties, were suddenly attacked in
very bad, broken and precipitous ground by very superior
numbers, who entirely outflanked them. The company first
drove the enemy before them, and took up an advantageous
position, but when they had to retire towards camp, it being
evening, the enemy followed them up, and, charging down
sword in hand (some of them coming as close as 30 yards),
endeavoured to secure a victory on their own rugged mountain
side, but the men, most gallantly led by Major Stewart and
Lieutenant Gaisford, met them with a countercharge, killed
two, and, wounding others, regained the crest they had just
left. The dash and spirit with which this was done so dis-
heartened the enemy that they at once drew off.

The casualties were three sepoys wounded—

Abdul Ghufar, very severely.
Muktiara,   ditto.
Hari Singh, slightly.

Major C. E. Stewart specially mentioned Lieutenant
Gaisford for his gallant and dashing conduct and for the
great assistance he rendered him. He also mentioned the very
forward and gallant behaviour of six men of the company—

Sepoy Abdul Ghufar, severely wounded.
  „   Said Shah.
  „   Lál Khan.
  „   Bassawah Singh.
  „   Urjoon.
  „   Phaugan.

All these men were recommended by a Military Court and by
the Brigadier-General Commanding for the Order of Merit,
and the three first mentioned have received the reward from
Government.

Movement
of the
force to
Camp
Shindeh.

On the 15th November 1877 the force retired from the
Paia Valley, and took up a position in the Turki Valley, facing
the pass leading to Jummoo. The regiment held the village

of Shere Ali and the heights by it, and which General Keyes considered the most exposed and important point in his whole position. This the regiment held from the 15th of November to the 7th of March, and, though the pickets and village were fired into and slightly attacked no less than seven times, there was only one casualty—Sepoy Dussu, E. Company, killed on the 20th November 1877. This was in a measure to be attributed to the strong and good breastworks which were built, and also to men scarcely even firing at the enemy, thereby not attracting the fire of the enemy towards themselves.

On the 1st December 1877 the regiment was attached to the right column of attack on the Jowáki stronghold of Jummoo, and, though it was well in advance, met with little opposition, and the men, driving the enemy rapidly before them, gave them no time to rally at any of the precipitous ridges which crossed the line of advance. When the force, three days subsequently, retired from Jummoo, the regiment was employed in covering the retirement on the right. Attack on Jummoo.

On the 7th December 1877 the regiment was attached to the right column of attack on the village of Ghariba. It marched from camp at 4 A.M., leading the advance, and when the high plateau beyond the village of Paia was gained the regiment, in conjunction with the 6th Punjab Infantry, rapidly advanced on Ghariba. Lieutenant Mein and Subadár-Major Aziz Khan, who were leading the skirmishers of the corps, pushed through the village, which the enemy did not attempt to hold, and seized the heights beyond, driving the enemy off them. A few prisoners were taken and a number of cattle. In the retirement the enemy did not attempt to follow up the right column. Attack on Ghariba.

On the 31st December 1877 the regiment formed a portion of the advance column which was, after occupying Ghariba, to ascend the Durgai heights and enable the main body to advance up the mountain path leading to the Wallai. This was carried out without opposition, and the regiment bivouacked that night on the Durgai. On the following day, when the whole force was retiring from that very high and precipitous mountain, the regiment had to cover the retirement. Lieutenant Gaisford with B. and D. Companies under Subadár-Major Aziz Khan had the most difficult duty of covering the final retirement from the heights. The enemy, who had mustered in force, and whose knowledge of the ground Ascent of the Durgai heights.

gave them a great advantage, attacked with great spirit, hoping from the nature of the ground to inflict heavy loss; but the abovementioned officers withdrew their men with such skill that there were no casualties, and the men themselves, in this the most difficult of all retirements, displayed conspicuously the soldier-like qualities of perfect coolness and obedience to orders under trying circumstances, and held their ground firmly against numbers with cool and quiet determination until ordered to withdraw. The regiment returned to Camp Shindeh that evening with the remainder of the force.

Advance on' Wallai and Naru Chini.

On the 15th of January 1878 the regiment with the 4th Punjab Infantry formed the right column on the second advance on the Durgai heights and range, and supported the advance up the mountain side of the 4th Punjab Infantry which was slightly opposed by the enemy. On the following day it was employed in the ascent of the opposite range of heights, and in the afternoon covered the retirement of the troops back to their Durgai bivouack.

On the 17th, 18th and 19th it took a prominent part in all the movements made in the neighbourhood of the Naru, and on the retirement of the force from the mountains was engaged in covering the retirement on the right flank.

It was then attached to Colonel Buchanan's Brigade at Jummoo, and formed the rear guard on the Brigade moving back to the camp at Shindeh.

In the advance on Jummoo, the attack on Ghariba, the ascent of the Durgai, and the final advance on Wallai and the Naru, the regiment was commanded by Major C. E. Stewart, as Major McQueen, the Commandant, had the command of one of the columns.

March to Kohat.

On the 7th of March 1878, on the conclusion of the hostilities, the regiment marched into Kohát in course of relief, where it was subsequently joined on the 8th of April by the wing from Abbott-abad under command of Captain C. M. Hall.

Extract of G. O. No. 738, dated Simla, 9th August 1878.

*   *   *   *   *   *

Thanks of Government.

" *Para.* 3. His Excellency in Council also desires to convey the acknowledgments of the Government of India to officers commanding corps, &c., &c., as well as to the officers, non-commissioned officers and men of the force, whose admirable behaviour and endurance during the

protracted and trying service merit the highest commendation. The
Governor-General in Council will have much pleasure in bringing the
services of all concerned to the favourable notice of Her Majesty's
Government."

Extract of letter No. 128 F. F., dated Abbott-abad, 8th March 1878.

"*Para.* 16. I now desire to bring to the notice of Government the
admirable conduct of the troops thoughout these operations. At Pain
the men not actually on duty had tolerably fair shelter, but immediately
after we had taken up new positions at Shindeh and Turki they were
exposed to thirty-six hours' rain with scarcely any shelter, and again not
many days afterwards seventy hours' almost continuous rain under
similar circumstances. They were without any change of clothes for
nearly a month; night duty was exceptionally heavy in consequence
of the extended nature of our position, yet the spirits of our men never
flagged, their cheerfulness and endurance under the hardships occasion-
ed by the unseasonable and unusually heavy rain was beyond all
praise."

"17. My hearty thanks and acknowledgments are due to all
the officers for their assistance, and for the excellent example which
they showed to the men by their own bearing throughout those
prolonged operations.

"18. My special thanks are also due to the following officers :—

*   *   *   *   *   *   *

"Major J. W. McQueen, Commandant, 5th Punjab Infantry. This
officer had charge of the eastern frontier blockade at Shádipore before
active operations commenced from the 19th to the 29th October 1877,
until the arrival of Colonel Gardiner, and was most useful in collecting
information in that quarter and in placing the exposed villages in a
state of defence. It was the good fortune of his regiment to hold the
most exposed and important point in the position taken up at Shindeh ;
and to the excellent arrangements of Major McQueen I am much indebted for the safety of that portion of the camp at Shindeh. Major
McQueen held command of the right column of attack on Jummoo and
in the advance on Ghariba, the assault of the Durgai heights and the
advance on Pustuwánai.

"No more important services were performed during the operations than those which fell to the lot of Major McQueen, and I cannot
speak in too high terms of the skill, spirit and dash with which these
important duties were performed. He merits my warmest acknowledgments for the assistance which he has rendered me throughout.

*   *   *   *   *   *   *

"The gallant actions performed by Major C. E. Stewart, 5th
Punjab Infantry, and Lieutenant G. Gaisford, 5th Punjab Infantry. on
and 15th November 1877   *   *   *   *   *   *

were described in my reports on the operations of those dates. I desire,
however, again to bring them to notice in this place. I cannot speak
too highly of those officers who have distinguished themselves by their
zeal and energy on all occasions.

"I have also to remark that Major C. E. Stewart commanded the
5th Punjab Infantry at the advance on Paia, Jamu, Ghariba, and
throughout the operations on the Durgai heights (on both occasions),
when the command of a separate column had devolved on the Commandant of the regiment. He fully earned the confidence of all ranks by the
coolness and skill which he invariably displayed."

Great sick-
ness in the
autumn of
1878. During the autumn of 1878 the regiment suffered very
severely from fever; there was scarcely a man in the ranks
who had not been in hospital three or four times. The
consequence was that on the 10th of October, when the
regiment marched on active service, what with this great
sickness, and there being a number of men on furlough, only
some 325 files could be mustered to march with regimental
head-quarters.

Increase to
regiment. On the 6th October 1878 orders were received to increase
the strength of the corps up to 800 privates, and men were at
once despatched to recruit the required number in the Punjab,
and as the British Government was going to war with the
Afgháns, no Patháns beyond the border were enlisted.

March to
Thull. On the 8th October 1878 the regiment received orders to
proceed to Thull by forced marches. It marched on the 10th
and reached Thull on the 13th, where it remained employed
in making roads, &c., until the 21st November, when war was
declared against Amír Sher Ali.

On that date the Kurram Field Force, under the command
of Major-General Roberts, v.c., c.b. (to the 1st Brigade of
which the regiment was attached), crossed the Kurram river,
and advanced up the valley of that name, viâ the Darwázágai
route, and arrived at Kurram Fort, 52 miles from Thull, without
meeting with any opposition.

Peiwar, 28th
November
1878. On the 28th November the whole force advanced towards
the Peiwar Kotal. The advanced guard was composed of the
5th Punjab Infantry, two guns, No. 2 Mountain Battery, and a
squadron of the 12th Bengal Cavalry, the whole under the
command of Major McQueen. When some five miles from the
enemy's position, the 5th Punjab Infantry, supported by the
29th Punjab Infantry and No. 2 Mountain Battery, were

directed to push up a narrow valley parallel to the Peiwar
Pass road, and after proceeding up this valley for some distance
to cross over the intervening spur and endeavour to capture
the enemy's guns, which they were said to be vainly endeavouring to drag up the pass. The regiment proceeded up the
valley and crossed the spur without any opposition, and nearly
succeeded in cutting off a portion of the enemy's rear-guard,
which were slowly retiring to their very strong position on the
range of heights over which the Peiwar Kotal road passes. As
the position held by the Afghán army was too strong to be
forced by only a portion of the force, the 5th Punjab Infantry
were halted under cover of the low mounds below the precipitous
heights held by the enemy, from which they soon began a
smart and galling fire. Shortly after this the 29th Punjab
Infantry, who had been following the 5th, advanced up
a deep and narrow gorge on the heights, to the north of which
they engaged the enemy, and being quite commanded from
the rocks above had to send for supports. On this Major
Pratt, taking with him six companies of the regiment, advanced
and afforded very material assistance, and with his men covered
the retirement of the troops with great judgment and skill ; in
this he was ably seconded by Captain Hall, Lieutenant Jameson,
and the Native Officers in command of companies.

In this affair of the 28th the following men were
wounded :—

> Subadár-Major Aziz Khan, Bahádur, very severely.
> Sepoy Kaim Khan, B. Company.
>   „ Ghulám Muhammad, ditto.
>   „ Jowáhir Singh, C. Company.
>   „ Miah Singh, A. Company.

Subadár-Major Aziz Khan, Bahádur, died on the 5th
January 1879 from the effects of the very severe wound
he had received, and the regiment lost in him one of the
finest and bravest Native Officers in the service, and the
Government a distinguished and loyal servant. The following Regimental Order, published after his death, bears testi-
mony to the esteem he was held in, and is a record of his
distinguished services :—

Subadár-Major Aziz Khan, Bahadur.

Regimental Order No. 201 A., dated 6th January 1879.

"It is with deep regret the Commanding Officer has to announce
the death at Kurram Fort on the 5th instant of Subadár-Major Aziz

Khan, Bahádur, from the effects of a severe gunshot wound received at
Peiwar on the 28th November 1878, and he desires to place on record
the very brilliant services of that gallant soldier, and at the same time
to acknowledge how much he was always personally indebted to
Subadár-Major Aziz Khan for his ready help, advice, and great tact
in the management of the men.

" All ranks in the regiment must feel their great loss in a leader
of such experience and cool and dashing courage, and one whose name
was proverbial amongst them for liberality and kindness, and whose
very distinguished conduct and services afford such a brilliant
example to all.

"Twice was Subadár-Major Aziz Khan decorated with the
Order of Merit for distinguished gallantry in the field ; he was also
awarded the Order of British India for long, good and faithful service,
as well as being given a turban of honor by Sir John Lawrence in
1857, and later on a dress and sword of honor by Sir Henry Davies,
Lieutenant-Governor of the Punjab."

WAR SERVICES.

Subadár-Major Aziz Khan, Bahádur, served at Mooltan in 1848
with the Levies under Sir Herbert Edwardes,—Medal. Miranzai
Expedition in 1856, North-West Frontier,—Medal and Clasp. Attack
on the mutinous 55th Regiment N. I. at Mardán, 25th May 1857.

Shaik Jana, 2nd July 1857. Narinjí, 21st July and 3rd August
1857. For distinguished gallantry on this last occasion he received a
turban of honor from Sir John Lawrence, Chief Commissioner, Punjab.
Oudh Campaigns of 1858-59, including actions of Bari, Simri, Nawáb-
ganj, and the forcing of the passage of the Goomtee river at Sultánpore :
operations on the Raptee under Lord Clyde, and several minor affairs
in the Nepal Terai in 1859,—Medal and 3rd Class of the Order of
Merit.

Umbeyla, 1863,—Clasp and 2nd Class of the Order of Merit.
Dress and sword of honor, 1873, for distinguished services, presented
by Sir Henry Davies, Lieutenant-Governor, Punjab. Jowáki-Afrídi,
1877-78.

Order of British India and title of Bahádur, 1878.

Afghán War. Kurram expedition under Major-General Roberts,
v.c., c.b. Peiwar, 28th November 1878, very severely wounded.

Peiwar, 2nd December 1878. For three days the force halted in front of the enemy's
very strong position in order to reconnoitre and see
whether it could not be turned. On the night of the 1st
December 1878 the main portion of the force, under personal command of the Major-General Commanding, marched

out of camp at 10 P.M., and after an extremely difficult and arduous night's march over very rugged and broken ground ascended by the Spin Gawai Pass and turned the left flank of the enemy, carrying at daybreak by storm the different stockades held by the Afghans on the mountain range, and drove them before them until brought to a stop by an almost impregnable position held in force by some regiments of the Amír's army. During these operations the column left behind in camp, of which the regiment formed a portion, marched out at daybreak to engage the enemy in front, and under instructions from Brigadier-General Cobbe, Commanding the 5th Punjab Infantry, ascended a long thickly-wooded spur, and was able to bring a heavy and effective fire on some of the enemy's guns and infantry. After the regiment had been committed to the advance up this spur, which ran parallel to the enemy's position, it was discovered that it was quite impossible to cross from it to the heights held by the Afgháns, as it was separated from them by a precipitous and quite impracticable gorge.

The regiment having ascended so far up the spur as to establish communications with the main column, Major McQueen was directed by the Major-General Commanding to bring up his regiment and take command of the advanced guard of a second turning movement, and had under his orders the 5th Goorkhas, 5th Punjab Infantry, and No. 1 Mountain Battery. This force was followed by the main body, the whole being under the Major-General Commanding. Without a shot being fired, this second turning movement was completely successful, and caused the enemy to evacuate their strong position, which was at once occupied by H. M.'s 8th, the King's, and other troops.

The force bivouacked for the night, some on the captured heights, and the main body far in advance at the upper end of the Hariáb Valley. The enemy were totally defeated, and all their guns (18), ammunition, supplies and camp equipage were captured.

The following morning the regiment brought into camp over fifty loads of shot and shell and small arm ammunition, besides discovering large quantities of grain and other supplies stored away for the use of the Afghán army in several of the villages of the Hariáb Valley.

These large collections of magazine stores and commissariat supplies evidently showed that the Afghans considered that they would be able to hold for certain their strong position against all assaults.

The following extract of demi-official No. 314 of the 4th December 1878 conveys the thanks of the Major-General Commanding to the troops under his command:—

"The Major-General Commanding congratulates the Kurram Field Force on the successful operations of the 2nd December 1878 against the Peiwar Kotal, a position of extraordinary strength, and held by an enemy resolute and well-armed.

"Not only had they advantage of ground, but also of numbers, as they were largely reinforced from Kabul the evening previous to the attack.

"A position apparently impregnable has been gained, a considerable portion of the Afghán army has been completely routed, and 18 guns with large stores of ammunition and supplies have been captured.

"The result is most honourable, and could only have been achieved by troops in a high state of discipline, capable of enduring great fatigue, and able to fight as soldiers of the British army have always fought. Major-General Roberts deeply regrets the brave men that have fallen in the gallant discharge of their duty, and feels much for the sufferings of the wounded."

Extract from despatch, dated Camp Zabardast Killa, 5th December 1878.

"I also desire to bring to special notice the name of Major McQueen, Commanding the 5th Punjab Infantry. This officer has passed his life on the frontier, and has great experience of the Patháns and of the best method of dealing with them. I have on many occasions found his assistance most valuable."

In the action of 2nd December the following men were wounded :—

Sepoy Jung Khan, B. Company.

„   Karrak Singh, F.   „

„   Taru,   H.   „

„   Asuf Khan, D.   „

Advance to Shutargardan and return to Kurram.

The regiment subsequently advanced to Ali Khel and Rokian, only a small party with Major McQueen accompanying the flying column to the Shutargardan. The regiment returned to the Kurram Fort on the 12th December 1878.

On the 24th December 1878 the regiment commenced its return march to Kohát, escorting all the captured guns, the sick, wounded, and a number of prisoners (21) sentenced by court-martial to long periods of penal servitude.

The regiment arrived at Kohát on the 4th of January, and left to rejoin the Kurram Field Force on the 6th March 1879. From October to March the regiment lost, principally from pneumonia bronchitis and dysentery upwards of 42 soldiers and 5 camp-followers. Such a heavy casualty list shows the arduous nature of the heavy duties the regiment had to perform, the fatigues the men had to undergo, as well as the extreme severity of the climate to which they were exposed. During this whole period nothing could be more exemplary than the conduct of the men, who at all times kept up the credit of the regiment by working well and cheerfully, although very much reduced by sickness.

At Thull, on the return march to Kohát, Lance Naick Ahmed Khan was shot when relieving sentries, and died within a few hours.

The regiment marched from Kohát for the Kurram Valley on the 6th March 1879, escorting ten lakhs of treasure, reaching Habib Killa on the 23rd of the same month, and occupied a portion of the old Afghán Cantonment.

On the 4th June 1879, 300 rifles were ordered to march to Keraya. On the 14th June 200 rifles were ordered to escort the Major-General towards the Bagiyar Pass. At about 8 miles from camp the escort was halted, and the Major-General with staff, accompanied by a few officers and orderlies, proceeded up the pass to visit the village of Lughi. *En route* this party was stopped, and subsequently attacked by the Mangals, and had to retire. On this occasion Havildár Hashim, B. Company, was severely wounded.

On the 16th June the regiment moved into camp near Shalozán in order to protect the workmen employed in laying out and building a cantonment and fort. From 20th June till 5th September 1879 the regiment was daily employed in levelling the ground and road-making in the new cantonment. The men also completed building barracks for two full companies ; cholera broke out whilst the regiment was employed on this duty, but fortunately it did not suffer much from this disease, only one out of six cases being fatal.

Return to Kohát.

Return to Kurram.

Keraya.

Building barracks and road-making at Shalosan.

Many men taking their discharge. During the months the regiment was at Shalozán, owing to the fact of all leave and furlough being stopped, and the men having hardly had any during the two previous years, many men took their discharge.

Attack on party near Gandiaur. On the 28th July 1879, while a party of furlough men, consisting of 2 Non-Commissioned Officers and 62 rank and file, were passing near Gandiaur on the Kohát and Thull road, they were suddenly attacked about 2 A.M. by a band of nearly 300 marauders, chiefly Ali Sherezais, Orakzais and Zaimushts. This party were escorting a number of carts, and were suddenly fired into from an ambush in the jungle about 15 yards from the road, and charged sword in hand by the Patháns. Thus suddenly attacked, the men had not time to load, but repelled the attack with the bayonet ; the Native Officer in command, Subadár Mirza Khan, and all his men behaving splendidly. It was a hand-to-hand fight ; three men were killed and nine wounded, all by the sword, and Subadár Mirza Khan, although wounded severely by a bullet in the first volley, gallantly headed his men in the fight, receiving two very severe sword-cuts. He subsequently, some months afterwards, died from the effects of these wounds.

The following men were killed and wounded in this affair :—

KILLED.

Naick Secunder Shah, D. Company.
Lance Naick Nuthu, B. Company.
Sepoy Kajir, G. Company.

WOUNDED.

Subadár Mirza Khan, E. Company ; since deceased.
Havildár Pasand Khan, B. Company.
Lance Havildár Panjaba, ditto ; since deceased.
   „   Naick Juffar, D. Company.
Sepoy Ganga Sing, ditto.
   „   Bahadur Singh, ditto.
   „   Wazír Singh, ditto.
Bugler Samunder, G. Company.

The enemy left two dead on the ground, and subsequent enquiries of the Deputy Commissioner, Kohát, elicited the information that two more had died from their wounds and some eight others had been wounded.

Six months' donation batta was granted to the regiment *Donation batta* for having taken part in this campaign.

On the 7th of September 1879 instructions were received *Advance to Shutargardan. Attack on posts and guard* from Divisional Head-Quarters to despatch 200 rifles under the command of a British Officer to Ali Khel and Karatiga. On the 8th a second telegram was received ordering a reinforcement for the above party of 100 rifles. In consequence of the massacre of the Kabul Embassy the Supreme Government having directed the advance on Kabul of General Sir Frederick Roberts's Division, the regiment received orders on the morning of the 16th September 1879 to march at once on Ali Khel, and on arrival there it was directed to push forward to the Shutargardan. Before the regiment reached the Shutargardan, Lieutenant McKinstry's party, which had gone on in advance, and was holding the Surkai Kotal and Karatiga posts in the Hazar Darakht defile, were attacked on the 22nd September, and repelled the Afghâns with the loss of only one man killed. On the same day a party of eight men in charge of Government mules and telegraph material were suddenly surrounded and attacked by overwhelming numbers whilst between these two posts, seven out of the eight men of the party being killed.

KILLED.

Lance Naick Prem Singh, A. Company.

Sepoy Boor Singh, C. Company.

  „ Habib, D. Company.

  „ Jumal Khan, ditto.

  · „ Balu, E. Company.

  „ Kalu, ditto.

  „ Gulab Singh, ditto.

  „ Ramzân, G. Company.

On the evening of the same day (22nd September 1879) the head-quarters of the regiment arrived and encamped at Karatiga. About 10 o'clock that night the Ghilzais and other Afghâns made an attack on the camp and pickets, and were after two hours' firing driven off.

The regiment reached the Shutargardan on the 23rd September and Khushi on the 26th, leaving *en route* 220 rifles under Captain Hall to hold the Surkai Kotal. While the army was collecting at Khushi, Amír Yakúb Khan with a large following came into camp and gave himself up.

All General Sir F. Roberts's Division having rendezvoused at Khushi by the 30th September, the army advanced towards Kabul.

Action of Charasiah. On the morning of the 6th October 1879 a wing of the regiment under Captain Hall, subsequently reinforced by 100 rifles under Lieutenant Sparling, took part in the attack on the Afghán position on the heights above Charásiah. At the critical moment when the enemy's centre had to be assaulted Captain Hall was directed to capture the key of the position : this he did, A. Company under Subadár Budh Singh leading the attack, and driving the enemy from their breastworks and killing many.

The following were the casualties in this attack :—

KILLED.

Jemadár Khani Mulla, D. Company.
Sepoy Labb Singh, C. Company.
    „   Ditta, E. Company.
Bugler Jai Ram, ditto.

WOUNDED.

Captain C. Young.
Sepoy Chuttar Singh, A. Company.
    „   Guran Ditta, E. Company ; since deceased.
    „   Sundar, ditto.
    „   Jowalla Singh, F. Company.

For his gallantry on this occasion Subadár Budh Singh received the Order of Merit.

Captain C. M. Hall was specially mentioned in General Baker's despatch, and subsequently again in Sir F. Roberts's.

Occupation of Kabul. On the evening of the 6th the head-quarters of the regiment with the remaining men were ordered to join General Baker; they came up with him late at night and bivouacked in the Sung-i-Nawishta Pass. The regiment remained without tents in this pass until the 9th, when it was ordered to march to the Siah Sung heights, and encamped with the rest of the force in the neighbourhood of Kabul. After taking part in General Sir F. Roberts's triumphal march through the streets of Kabul the regiment was ordered off as part of a force under Brigadier-General Hugh Gough to relieve the troops on the Shutargardan, who were surrounded by immense numbers of the Ghilzais and other Afghán clans.

The Shutargardan was reached on the 20th October without any opposition, the enemy having fled on the approach of General Gough's force. On the 23rd the Shutargardan was abandoned, and the force marching down the Logar Valley returned to Kabul on the 4th November 1879.

Lines were assigned to the regiment at Sherpur Cantonments, and the men had to work in enclosing the arches of the verandahs of the Afghán barracks and in building cook-houses, guard-rooms, bazár, and officers' quarters. Bricks had to be carried some distance, and all timber for roofing brought by the men on their shoulders from the Bála Hissar, a distance of some 3 miles. All this time guard and other fatigue duties, such as demolishing buildings in the Bála Hissar and foraging, were very heavy. *Building lines.*

On the 14th November 1879 a sick convoy was despatched to India, and Major McQueen, Captain Young, Lieutenant McKinstry, Subadár-Major Pír Shah, and many of the sick and wounded were sent with it.

On the 9th November a detachment of 100 rifles under Captain Hall was sent to hold Butkhak, and held that place until the 30th.

On the 21st November the regiment formed part of a force under Brigadier-General Baker which went to Maidán to forage and survey the country, and as some foraging parties in Upper Maidán were fired upon by the villagers, several walled villages were burnt and destroyed. The force returned to Kabul on the 1st December 1879. *First visit to Maidán.*

On the 9th December 1879 the regiment again accompanied Brigadier-General Baker towards Maidán, marching *vid* the Logar Valley. That afternoon the regiment encamped at Childukteran, and on the following morning, the 10th, marched for Maidán, 100 rifles under Lieutenant Sparling forming the rear-guard. On that night the rear-guard being delayed by the great difficulties of the road through the pass, and the march being an extremely long one, was unable to reach General Baker's camp in the Maidán Valley, and had to bivouac for the night in the pass. The night was a bitterly cold one, and no fires could be lighted in consequence of the proximity of the enemy ; the men suffered severely. *Second visit to Maidán.*

On the morning of the 11th the troops marched off immediately on the appearance of the rear-guard, which had to fight its way into camp in the morning, General Baker's intention being to co-operate with General Macpherson's force against the enemy, known to be in camp at Arghandeh. When the troops had marched, and the rear-guard, the same 100 men under Lieutenant Sparling, was also leaving the ground, the enemy debouched in great numbers from the very same pass on which the rear-guard had passed the night ; they also came in large numbers from the Ghazni direction, threatening to cut off the rear-guard, and attacked with great perseverance. Lieutenant Sparling having to send for reinforcements, another 100 of the regiment under Lieutenant Jameson and two mountain guns were sent to his assistance ; unitedly they drove off the enemy. The force encamped that night at Arghandeh.

On the head of the column reaching the encamping ground, some hills in front had to be cleared of some small bodies of the enemy ; this was effected chiefly by artillery.

The casualties of the regiment on this day were as follows :—

KILLED.

Sepoy Muhammad Yar, B. Company.

WOUNDED.

Sepoy Nihal Singh, C. Company.

„ Sohail Singh, F. Company ; since deceased.

„ Wasim, G. Company ;   ditto.

„ Muhammad Ali, D. Company.

Bhisti Bhagu, C. Company ; since deceased.

On this occasion Naick Sarwan Singh, C. Company, received the Order of Merit for gallantry in the field.

Arghandeh to Katul, 12th December 1879.
On the force preparing to march on the morning of the 12th December 1879, the standards of the enemy were seen on the Tukt in Kotal and other hills in rear of the camp.

The combination movement with General Macpherson having failed, General Baker was required with his force in Kabul. On the troops being moved off General Baker placed the rear-guard, consisting of the 5th Punjab Infantry, 1 squadron 5th Punjab Cavalry and two mountain guns, under Major Pratt. As the main body of General Baker's force moved off the enemy began the attack on the rear-guard. Two companies were thrown forward to occupy ground near the advancing enemy, and held them in check until the baggage had got well away. The rear-guard then began to retire slowly. This was a signal for the advance of the enemy, who came on on both flanks and along the ravines in the centre of the valley. To prevent being outflanked, a company was detached to the left under Subadár Budh Singh ; the guns assisted the retirement, and the men retired as steadily and slowly as on parade, and effectually prevented the Afgháns from closing on the baggage. After following up for nearly six miles the enemy desisted from pressing the rear-guard. The regiment had only one sepoy wounded on this occasion—Saif Ali, B. Company.

In these two rear-guard affairs the enemy are believed to have lost 37 men in killed alone.

Major Pratt was specially mentioned in despatches for having ably commanded the rear-guard.

On the 13th December 1879 the regiment was broken up into several detachments, one party of 150 rifles under Major Pratt being ordered to open out communications with Brigadier-General Baker's force, which was operating against the enemy beyond the Bála Hissar. This was done successfully, and in performance of this duty a party of the enemy were encountered near the city walls posted under cover of some embankments and willow trees. They were immediately attacked, driven from their positions and pursued. Twenty of the enemy's dead were counted. On this occasion Lieutenant Jameson particularly distinguished himself, killing two of the enemy. On reaching General Baker's force the party under Major Pratt was ordered to take a fortified serai still occupied by the enemy. The gate of this serai was set on fire by piling grass, &c., against it. The occupants, however, maintained for a time a smart musketry fire from the walls, until the place was surrounded, when the men opened such a well-directed fire on the walls that the enemy at last could not show their heads with impunity above them to fire. To dislodge the defenders ladders had to be brought from a village close by, and placed against a wall discovered to be free from buildings, allowing the men to defend it. Volunteers were called for by Major Pratt to ascend these ladders. The call was

Sherpur, 13th December 1879.

readily responded to and men mounted them, rifles being
handed to them by their comrades, and the Afgháns on the
wall opposite being taken in reverse were speedily dislodged.
The defenders then came for the cover under the wall against
which the scaling ladders were, and kept throwing over
showers of stones on the men on the ladders, dislodging one
man and bruising others. It was then decided to take the
place by assault, as the door of the serai had now been burnt
down. Major Pratt led the assaulting party, but just on entering the gateway, Havildár Shám Singh gallantly rushed past
him, was fired into and attacked by the Afgháns on both sides
of the gateway, receiving one bullet wound and five sword-
cuts. The defenders of the place were soon overpowered.
The following were the casualties :—

WOUNDED.

Havildár Shám Singh, A. Company ; since deceased.

Sepoy Kurban Ali, D. Company.

,,   Assa Singh, A. Company.

,,   Awal Khan, D. Company.

The following men were recommended and received the
Order of Merit :—

Subadár Baz Gul,   D. Company.

Lance Naick Akram,   ditto.

Sepoy Oomrah,   ditto.

Lance Naick Niamat,   ditto.

Lance Naick Mán Singh, A. Company.

Asmai
heights, 14th
December
1879.

On the 14th December 1879 the regiment marched out
with the force under Brigadier-General Baker to attack the
enemy collected in great numbers on the Koh Asmai heights
above Deh-Afghána, a suburb of Kabul. The regiment was
in rear of the column, and was halted on its arrival at the
position selected by the General for the reserve and from
which to direct the operation. The place chosen by General
Baker was a ridge with three strong-walled enclosures, called
Killa Biland. In the left enclosure 25 men under Lieutenant Sparling were placed ; in the centre one 25 men under
Lieutenant Onslow, R.E. ; and in the right 25 under a Native
Officer. In addition to the above 25 rifles more were told off
as an escort to G-8 Royal Artillery. At about 11-30 A.M. an
escort of 100 rifles of the regiment, placed by the special
order of Brigadier-General Baker under the command of

Lieutenant Wilson, Xth Hussars, was directed to accompany No. 2 Mountain Battery to a conical hill on the opposite range, about a mile distant, held by detachments of the 72nd Highlanders and Guides, under the command of Colonel Clarke, 72nd Highlanders. Shortly after 12 o'clock the enemy made a determined attack in great force on this position, driving our own troops off it in great confusion. General Baker seeing the troops giving way despatched 100 men under Captain Hall to reinforce them, but before this officer could reach the position, it had been lost, and at the same time two of our mountain guns which had been abandoned.

Captain Hall with his small party pushed past our retreating soldiers, and endeavoured to give them encouragement to rally by leading his party up the hill. He succeeded in gaining the top, but was unable to hold it against the overwhelming numbers who came up against him, flushed with their previous success. He and his men then slowly retired off the hill, covering the withdrawal of the remaining guns, and subsequently took up such a position at the base of the hill that he effectually checked the advance of the enemy down into the plain.

Captain Hall's arrangements both in advancing and retiring off the hill were most judicious, his own cool and forward conduct tending to keep his men well together and in hand, and ending in checking the further advance of the enemy in that part of the field. Captain Hall reports most favourably of the gallantry and conduct throughout the whole of this most trying affair of Subadár Juma Khan, H. Company, a Native Officer who has never failed to distinguish himself whenever opportunity offered.

The casualties on this occasion were—

KILLED.

Sepoy Buddu, E. Company.

WOUNDED.

Havildár Harif, H. Company.
Naick Hussun, B. Company.
    „   Ruldu, E. Company ; since deceased.
    „   Chanda Singh, A. Company.
Sepoy Núr Khan, B. Company.
    „   Emam Bakhsh, H. Company.

Sepoy Ghanta, E. Company.

„ Mehtab, B. Company.

„ Aga Rám, E. Company.

„ Kasim, B. Company; since deceased.

„ Lál Singh, C. Company;   ditto.

„ Kaudu, E. Company.

„ Hera,   ditto.

On the retirement of the troops into Sherpur that evening, the 5th Punjab Infantry covered the withdrawal of
General Baker's brigade.

Siege of
Sherpur.
The siege of Sherpur commenced from the night of the
14th and lasted till the 23rd, a period of nine days. The
men slept in the defences every night, ready to man the walls
at a moment's notice On the 15th and 16th the defences
were strengthened. On the 17th Major Pratt was ordered
with a wing of the regiment to clear the King's garden (5th
Punjab Cavalry quarters).

This garden had been shelled from Sherpur previous to
the advance of the wing, and was taken with hardly any opposition, there being only one casualty — Sepoy Darbári wounded.
On the 18th a detachment of 150 rifles under Lieutenant Mein
was ordered to hold the King's garden. During the whole of
that day the enemy kept up a smart fire on the garden, but
Lieutenant Mein only lost one man, Sepoy Dewah Singh,
C. Company, killed, as the "Shah Bagh," King's garden, was
a strong walled enclosure, and gave excellent cover. On the
· 23rd the Afgháns under their leaders, General Mahomed Jan
and Mulla Muski Alam, made their final attack on the Sherpur lines, and were repulsed and dispersed, the casualties in the
regiment being—

KILLED.

Syce Kishan Singh.

WOUNDED.

Sepoy Esar Singh, F. Company.

„ Sharm Singh,   ditto.

On the evening of the 23rd General Sir F. Roberts or-
dered a small chosen party of 10 Sikhs and 10 Afrídís, under
Suhadár Juma Khan, to reconnoitre in the dusk Mahomed
Sharíf's fort, which is not far from the Sherpur Cantonment,

and which was reported to be held by the enemy. Subadár Juma Khan and his party, taking advantage of its being dusk, not only reconnoitred the place, but, seeing that the Afgháns were not on the look-out, suddenly rushed one of the walls ; the Afgháns in the place being taken quite by surprise fled, not knowing the smallness of the attacking party. Four of the men were killed, and three fully caparisoned horses were captured. General Sir F. Roberts was much pleased with Subadár Juma Khan's conduct and leading on this occasion, and thanked him personally, and on his recommendation received the 2nd Class of the Order of Merit. Havildárs Sher Dín and Barám Khan-both distinguished themselves by their forward behaviour on this occasion.

On the 24th the regiment occupied the city, and the place was held that night by detachments of the regiment under Captain Hall, who had possession of the Kotwáli and the Lahore Gate of the city.

On the 27th December the regiment formed a portion of the force that marched for the Koh-i-Daman. At Baba Kuch Kai three of Mír Batcha's forts were blown up, his fruit trees ringed and vineyards destroyed, the force returning to Sherpur on the 31st December. This march was very trying for the troops, snow lying thick on the ground, cold intense, and camp and picket duties very severe. *March to Koh-i-Daman.*

Working parties of the regiment were daily employed during January and February 1880 in levelling all the walled enclosures round Sherpur and in strengthening the defences.

The conduct of the men all through this trying winter was admirable, and the regiment had its full share of hard work, and did it well and cheerfully.

On the 8th May 1880 the regiment, under Lieutenant-Colonel McQueen, accompanied General Sir F. Roberts's division in its march through the Logar Valley, Wardak and Maidán. From Maidán the 2nd Goorkha Regiment and the 5th Punjab Infantry marched back to Kabul through the Lalándár defiles, following the course of the Kabul river—a very mountainous and rugged country, which had hitherto been unexplored—arriving at Sherpur on 1st June. *March through Logar, Wardak and Maidan.*

From this date until the 6th August 1880 detachments of the regiment were constantly employed in protecting

convoys on the line of communications. On the 6th August the
regiment paraded before Lieutenant-General Sir F. Roberts,
who presented Orders of Merit to the Native Officers and men
who had gained that reward, and the Lieutenant-General was
then pleased to express his approbation of the behaviour of the
regiment both in the field and in quarters during the past two
years whilst serving under his command. On the same day
the regiment moved into the Bála Hissar to garrison it, and
also took over the pickets on the Sher Darwáza heights.

Evacuation of Kabul   On the 11th August 1880 the troops under Sir Donald
Stewart evacuated Kabul, the 5th Punjab Infantry being the
last to be withdrawn from the Bála Hissar, the Officer Commanding, Lieutenant-Colonel McQueen, making over the keys
of that fortress to Amír Abdul Rahmán's representatives.
The return march of the troops to the Punjab was without
accident, the regiment reaching its station, Kohat, on the 10th
September 1880.

The following is a return of the casualties of the regiment
during the Afghán campaigns of 1878-79-80 :—

	British Officers.	Native Officers.	N. C. Officers.	Rank & File.	Followers.	Total
Killed	...	3	5	21	2	31
Wounded	1	...	5	34	...	40
Died	...	...	11	69	7	87
Total	1	3	21	124	9	158

In the Afghán despatches of Lieutenant-General Sir F.
Roberts the following officers were mentioned :—

Extract from Despatch dated 22nd October 1879.

"I have the honor to submit an abridged list of those whose services have been most particularly marked and valuable :—

*   *   *   *

Major J. W. McQueen, 5th Punjab Infantry. It is possible that
Majors McQueen, FitzHugh and Galbraith may have been recommended
for some reward in the late campaign. I trust, however, it will not be
considered out of place if I bring their names forward for some further
reward. Nothing can exceed the good services performed by Majors
McQueen and FitzHugh, and also by their distinguished regiment."

Extract from Despatch No. 1027, dated 23rd January 1880.

"*Para.* 45. During this day, the 12th December, General Baker's
brigade returned to Sherpur. The enemy showed themselves in consider-

nble force in his rear and on both flanks, and the rear-guard, which was
ably commanded by Major H. M. Pratt, 5th Punjab Infantry, was at
first closely pressed.

"93. The following officers one and all deserve my thanks for
their good services :—

    *   *   *   *

Captain Hall.

Captain C. M. Hall, 5th Punjab Infantry."

In the same despatch the gallant conduct of Jemadár
Abdul Rahmán and Havildár Shám Singh (since deceased)
were prominently noted by the Lieutenant-General Commanding.

Jemadar Abdul Rahman, Havildar Sham Singh.

Subadár-Major Pír Shah was admitted to the 2nd class
of the Order of British India, with the title of " Bahádur," by
G. G. O. No. 579 of 1880, with effect from the 2nd November
1879, for his long and distinguished services.

Subadar-Major Pir Shah, Bahadur, Order of British India.

On the 5th February 1881 the regiment marched for the
Miranzai Valley, head-quarters halting at Togh, where it formed part of the Kurram Brigade Field Force under General J.
Gordon, and detachments of the regiment occupied the outposts of Thull, Gundiaur and Surozai until the 16th April,
when they rejoined head-quarters, the regiment having received orders to march to Bannu and join the 2nd column of
the Wazíri Field Force. On the 4th May this column
advanced by the Kasura route into the Wazíri country,
reaching Razmak, in the heart of that country, on the 9th
of May. After halting there for four days it returned by the
Shuktu route, reaching British territory on the 20th May.
The column met with no opposition, but the troops were
actively employed the whole time in making reconnaissances,
guarding survey parties, foraging and road-making.

Regiment marches to join Kurram Brigade

Mahsud Waziri Expedition 1881.

On the 10th May a detachment of two British Officers and
150 rank and file formed portion of a strong party under the
command of Major C. M. Hall, 5th Punjab Infantry, sent to
escort the surveyors to the top of the Shewidhur mountain —
one of the highest peaks in Wazíristán, being upwards of
11,000 feet high. On the 11th, whilst this party was retiring down the mountain, it was attacked, and the rear-guard, composed of men of the 5th Punjab Infantry detachment, steadily
covered the retirement without losing a man themselves, and
killing five of the enemy, capturing their arms. On this
occasion Jemadár Abdul Rahmán distinguished himself.

The following officers were specially mentioned in General Gordon's despatch of the 26th May 1881 :—

"I beg to bring to the favourable notice of the Brigadier-General Commanding the Force the services of the following officers and those under their command :—

＊　　＊　　＊　　＊

Lieutenant-Colonel J. W. McQueen, c.b., 5th Punjab Infantry.

Major C. M. Hall, 5th Punjab Infantry.

"Lieutenant-Colonel J. W. McQueen, c.b., Commandant, 5th Punjab Infantry, performed very valuable services as Commandant of the Out-posts. Under his orders the posting of pickers in the most suitable positions for the protection of the camps by day and night, and along the line of march, was ably secured."

Return to Kohat. On the 27th May 1881 the regiment returned to cantonments at Kohát after an absence of three and a half months.

Thanks of Government. The services of the regiment during the Mahsúd-Wazíri Expedition were acknowledged by the Governor-General in Council in his letter No. 2635B., dated Simla, 8th August 1881, to the Adjutant-General in India, in which his thanks were conveyed to the whole force.

Distinction of corps. The following extract from G. G. O. No. 418 of 29th July 1881 is published :—

"The Most Hon'ble the Governor-General in Council announces that Her Majesty the Queen-Empress of India has been graciously pleased to permit the following corps to bear upon their standards, colors, or appointments the words specified below in commemoration of their gallant conduct during the recent campaigns in Afghánistán:—

5th Punjab Infantry { 'Peiwar Kotal;' 'Charásiah;' 'Kabul, 1879;' 'Afghánistán, 1878-80.' "

Order of British India. The following extract of G. G. O. No. 571 of 21st October 1881 is published :—

"In recognition of their services during the late war in Afghánistán, His Excellency the Governor-General in Council is pleased to admit the undermentioned Native Officers to the 1st and 2nd Class of the Order of British India with effect from the 21st October 1881 :—

1st Class, Subadár-Major Pír Shah, to 'Sirdár Bahádur.'

2nd Class, Subadár Juma Khan, to 'Bahádur.'"

Inspection of regiment. The regiment was inspected by General T. G. Kennedy, c.b., on the 2nd December 1881.

On the 17th December 1881 the regiment marched from Kohát for Dera Ismail Khan, arriving at the latter station on the 3rd January 1882. *Change of station.*

By G. G. O. No. 210 of 22nd April 1882 the regiment was increased in strength by the addition of 80 privates, *viz.*, from 640 to 720. *Augmentation of strength.*

On the 23rd January 1882 the regiment was inspected by His Honor the Lieutenant-Governor of the Punjab. *Inspection by His Honor the Lieutenant-Governor.*

The regiment was inspected by Brigadier-General T. G. Kennedy, C.B., on the 1st February 1882. *Inspection by Brigadier-General T. G. Kennedy.*

The regiment was inspected by Brigadier-General T. G. Kennedy, C.B., on the 27th February 1883. *1883.*

On the 14th November 1883 the head-quarters and five hundred bayonets marched towards Draband to form part of the escort accompanying a survey party to the Takht-i-Sulemán. *Marches for the Takht-i-Suleman.*

26th *November* 1883.—One hundred and eighty rifles under Major C. M. Hall took part in the front attack of the Párzai Kotal, and the same number of men joined the right attack ; the latter were commanded by Major A. D. Strettell. The front attack occupied 2¾ hours from 6 A.M., and the right or flank attack 6 hours from 2-30 A.M., to a circuit of about 6 miles and the ascent of the mountain. *Occupation of Parzai Kotal.*

The regiment returned to Dera Ismail Khan on the 8th December 1883. *Return to Dera Ismail Khan.*

15th *January* 1884.—The regiment was inspected by His Honor the Lieutenant-Governor of the Punjab, Sir Charles Aitchison, also by Brigadier-General T. G. Kennedy, C.B., on the 23rd February 1884. *1884. Inspection by His Honor the Lieutenant-Governor and by Brigadier-General.*

Assistant Adjutant-General's No. 278, dated 8th May 1884, conveyed the thanks of the Government of India to the troops composing the Takht-i-Suleman Expedition of November and December 1883. For loss owing to wear and tear of clothing Government granted Rs. 5 to each fighting man and Rs. 3 to each public follower. Free rations were not sanctioned. *Acknowledgment by Government of services in the Takht-i-Suleman Expedition. Government letter No. 31 S.B., dated 18th April 1884, to Punjab Military.*

Printed report of the Takht-i-Suleman Expedition.

On the 3rd July 1884 were received for record the printed reports of the Takht-i-Suleman Expedition, containing (a) the report by the Punjab Government ; (b) the despatch by the General Officer in Command ; (c) subsidiary reports by Colonel McLean on the front attack of the Parzai Kotal, and the crowning of the "Obas Kai," or highest peak of the northern end of the Takht, and (d) by Colonel Rice on the flank march and attack ; and (e) reports on the route and the mountain by the Quartermaster of the Force, Captain Radford.

The following notes of interest are entered from these reports :—

Route.

Border crossed on 18th November 1883 from Kot Lalu. Sheoráni country entered through Shek Haidar Pass.

Note on Zao Tangi, 5,750 feet above sea-level.

* Kot Guldád,	11 miles.
Gundari Kach.	13 „
Zao Tangi Sir,	6 „
Mazrai Kach,	13 „
Wazhdan,	9 „
Parzai or Pazai	4 „

Parzai springs reached in six marches.* Two days were spent in passing the Zao defile, one in making the road, and another in passing the supplies and baggage along it. Most of the animals had to be unladen and laden on either side of a large rock which blocks the road known as the "Sari" rock, height 30 feet, resting on other rocks 10 feet high, chasm 28 feet wide. Waterfalls on either side of the rock from a height of 30 feet. The right fall is straight, but the left is over a succession of rocks and boulders. To pass camels, the stream was diverted into the right channel, and a ramp was made from the bed of the stream to the top of the fall on the left bank. These ramps were made of stones and grass topped with sand.

Transport. Survey of the Obas Kai or Kaisar Ghar Peak.

Transport of force, mules only. Fifteen days' supplies on hill camels hired from Powindahs. Four days' more supplies were met the force on the return march.

When the Parzai Kotal was carried on 26th November arrangements were made for moving on. On 27th November a reconnaissance was made seven miles to Maidán, a small level connecting the parallel ridges of the mountain and forming the water-shed of the Drabaud and Chaudwan Zams.

On the 28th the survey party, men only, marched for Maidán from Parzai Kotal.† It was divided into a summit party, 200 rifles—each man 50 rounds, 1 poshtin, 1 tin of water, 1 day's food.

† 8,600 feet above sea-level.

(a) No. 9-54, dated 8th January 1884.
(b) No. 104 C. B.. dated 14th December 1883.
(c) Dated 2nd December 1883.
(d) Dated 26th November 1883.
(e) Dated 6th December 1883.

Carrying party—200 rifles, 20 rounds each man, one poshtin, 2 days' provisions, and 2 days' water in small mussucks and tins. Followers also were used to carry water.

On the 29th November the carriers returned to Parzai springs, and the survey and summit party marched from Maidán, 4 miles, to Gangsar at the foot of the Obas Kai peak, which is 2,300 feet above Gangsar and 11,300 above the sea. The summit was reached at 12-30 noon. Gangsar was reached again before dark.

On the 30th November the party marched back to Maidán and Parzai Kotal, and on the 1st December all parties were collected at Parzai springs below the Kotal.

This survey was performed without bedding in great cold.

The following extracts from the reports by Colonel McLean and the Brigadier-General show the kind of work which fell to the troops :—

Extract from report by Colonel McLEAN.

" The men willingly gave up their bedding, and submitted to many discomforts in order that the objects of the expedition might be attained. Their shoes, which had been already much damaged by the water of the Zao Pass, suffered severely from the exceeding roughness of the rocks of the Takht, and their clothes were torn by the bushes through which our march lay. Owing to the absence of bedding they were at night obliged to huddle close up to the fires, and in this way their poshtins, turbans and clothing got burned, and were much damaged by the thick black smoke emitted by the pine-wood fire."

Extract from report by Brigadier-General T. G. KENNEDY.

" To account for these losses were the rough and stony marches, with much wading of water, carrying camel and mule loads through a block in the Zao Pass, severe hill-climbing, carrying mussucks of water for various distances up to 7 miles, heavy escort duties, pickets, bivouacs and otherwise, sitting in the very cold nights close over pine-wood fires with their dense black smoke and flying sparks, and every man in camp had the rough marches and cold nights, and nearly all their full share of the other duties and exposure."

Letter No. 108 C.B., dated 14th December 1883.

On the 20th December 1884 the regiment marched in relief from Dera Ismail Khan to Edwardesabad, arriving at Edwardesabad on the 26th December 1884 under Colonel A. G. Ross, Officiating Commandant, and relieving the 4th Sikh Infantry. The regiment occupied the Fort Dalipgarh Lines in the main fort, having two companies quartered in the Cavalry Lines for sanitary reasons. Marching in strength on 30th December 1884, four Native Officers and 130 Non-Commissioned Officers and rank and file marched in from Deraját outposts.

Change of stations, 1884.

6 British Officers.
9 Native Officers.
577 Non-Commissioned Officers and rank and file.

Transport completed on scale of 1882.

On 19th December 1884 the regiment received its two light carts (carriage capability of each 12 maunds) ; these completed the scale of transport under the scheme of 1882, making 50 camels, 58 mules and 2 light carts, estimated for a wing equipped for field service. The 58 mules include mules (5) for pakalis.

1885. Inspection by Lieutenant-Governor.

On the 17th January 1885 the regiment, as a portion of the Edwardesabad Brigade, was inspected by Sir Charles Aitchison, Lieutenant-Governor of the Punjab.

Inspection by Brigadier-General Commanding Punjab Frontier Force.

On the 26th February 1885 the regiment was inspected by Brigadier-General T. G. Kennedy, c. b., and also in brigade and field firing beyond Gumathi on the 2nd March 1885 with the Bannu Brigade. Seventy-one men were in hospital, chiefly from fever, but in every other respect the Brigadier-General reported the regiment very efficient and fit for service.

Old colours. Disposal.

In letter No. $\frac{164}{Q. M.}$, dated 12th November 1884, application was made by Colonel A. G. Ross for permission to send the old colors of the regiment to the Lawrence Hall in Lahore. The colors were of the old large pattern with spearheads on the poles, the pattern in use till after the Indian Mutiny. The regiment had never carried its colors, and never replaced the old colors originally issued. Sanction was accorded in No. 101 C., dated 5th February 1885, which forwarded the consent of the Municipal Committee of Lahore (No. 2, dated 14th January 1885) to receive the colors for deposit in the Lawrence Hall. The old colors were left in charge of Color Havildár Hira Singh, F. Company, on 21st March 1885 (R. O. No. 350 of 21st March 1885), and were duly delivered over to the Deputy Commissioner of Lahore for transfer to the Municipal Committee.

Transfer of transport animals owing to formation of army corps to resist Russia.

In April 1885, owing to the aggressive action of Russia on the western borders of Afghánistán, orders were issued for the mobilisation of two army corps. The regiment was not detailed for either. By Assistant Adjutant-General's telegram No. 25, dated 13th April 1885, 38 camels and 33 mules, with attendants and equipment complete, were permanently transferred to the 4th Punjab Infantry at Dera Ghází Khan, and by telegram No. 55, dated 20th April 1885, 8 camels and 5 mules to the 1st Sikh Infantry at Dera Ismail Khan. These animals left on 21st and 29th April 1885 respectively, leaving the corps with only fragments of transport. The transfers are to be replaced by regimentally arranged purchases.

In October the whole of the transports transferred to the 1st Sikh Infantry and 4th Punjab Infantry were returned to the regiment by Assistant Adjutant-General's No. 566 M. R., dated Abbott-abad, September 23rd, 1885.

Transport returned.

The order to purchase transport animals regimentally was cancelled by Assistant Adjutant-General's telegram No. 168, dated Abbott-abad, 9th May 1885.

Cancelling purchase of transport animals regimentally.

On the 26th February 1886 the regiment was inspected in drill order by Brigadier-General Sir C. M. MacGregor, K.C.B., Commandant, Punjab Frontier Force.

1886. Inspection.

On the 1st March 1886 the regiment was seen by the Brigadier-General Commanding at ball firing on the rifle range, also at skirmishing drill, and on the 2nd of March at a brigade field-day near Gumathi Pass.

Sir C. MacGregor expressed himself as being much pleased with the fine appearance of the regiment and at the steadiness of the men on parade (*vide* Regimental Order No. 155, dated 3rd March 1886).